lecool

A WEIRD AND WONDERFUL
GUIDE TO LONDON

First published by LE COOL Publishing SL
www.lecool.com

Designed at John Brown
www.johnbrowngroup.co.uk

Printed in Barcelona, Spain by Novo Print
on paper manufactured from sustainable forests

ISBN 978-84-612-3227-7

We chose this city.

We came here in a Transit, the rest of the band asleep on the flight cases in the back.

We quit law school and came here to work in our uncle's restaurant, saving a little money here, a little money there.

We took the sleeper from Glasgow for the weekend, snuck in to Boombox, promised each other on the platform on the way back up that next time we came down it'd be for good.

We came here in a borrowed suit and our funeral tie to be interviewed for that big-money job in the City.

We came to study here because it's London, not for the course or the college.

We came to graffiti the trains at Willesden Junction one night, met some people, got a job in an art supplies shop and ripped up our return ticket.

We came for the boys. We came for that girl.

We came to do shitty jobs Monday to Friday and live like stars Saturday and Sunday.

We came here because of Jeffrey Bernard, or Jazzy B, or Johnny Rotten.

We came here so we could dress how we like, love who we like, be who we like.

The myths are all true. Dragons stalk the city, the streets are paved with gold. There are angels in Peckham Rye and paradise is by way of Kensal Green.

We're here because we choose to be. This is our London.

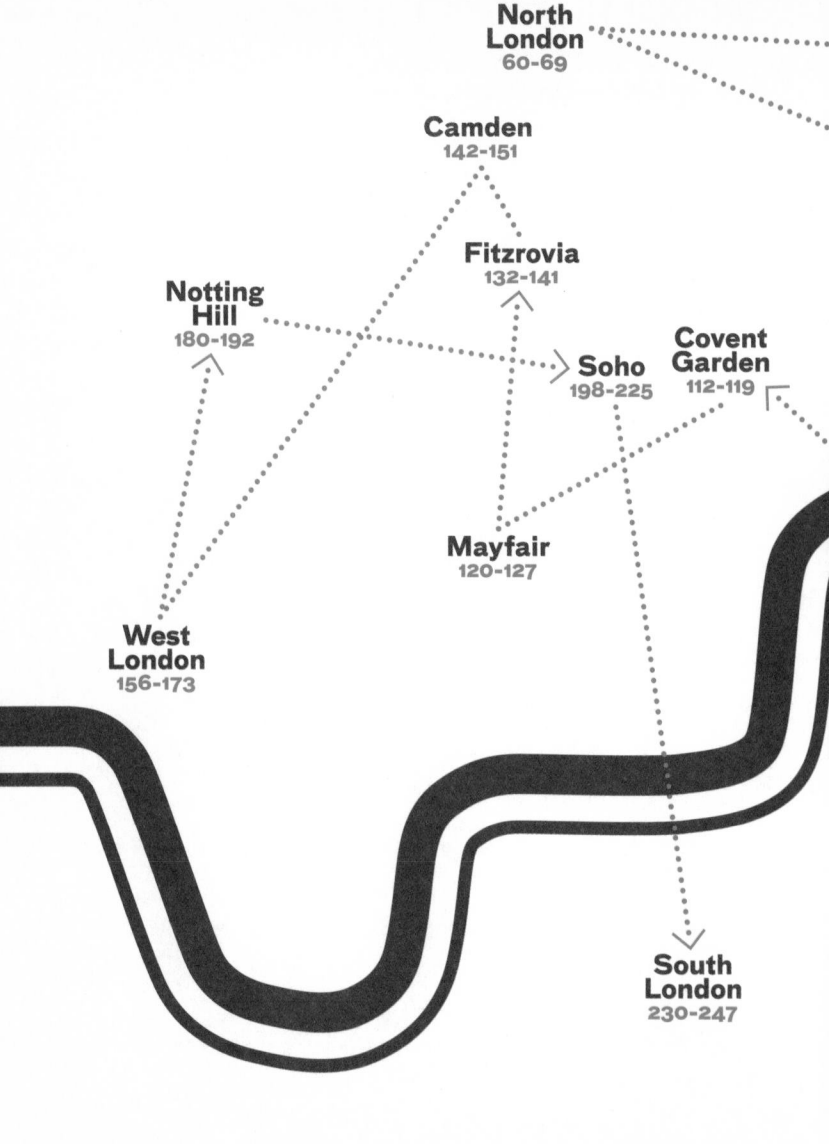

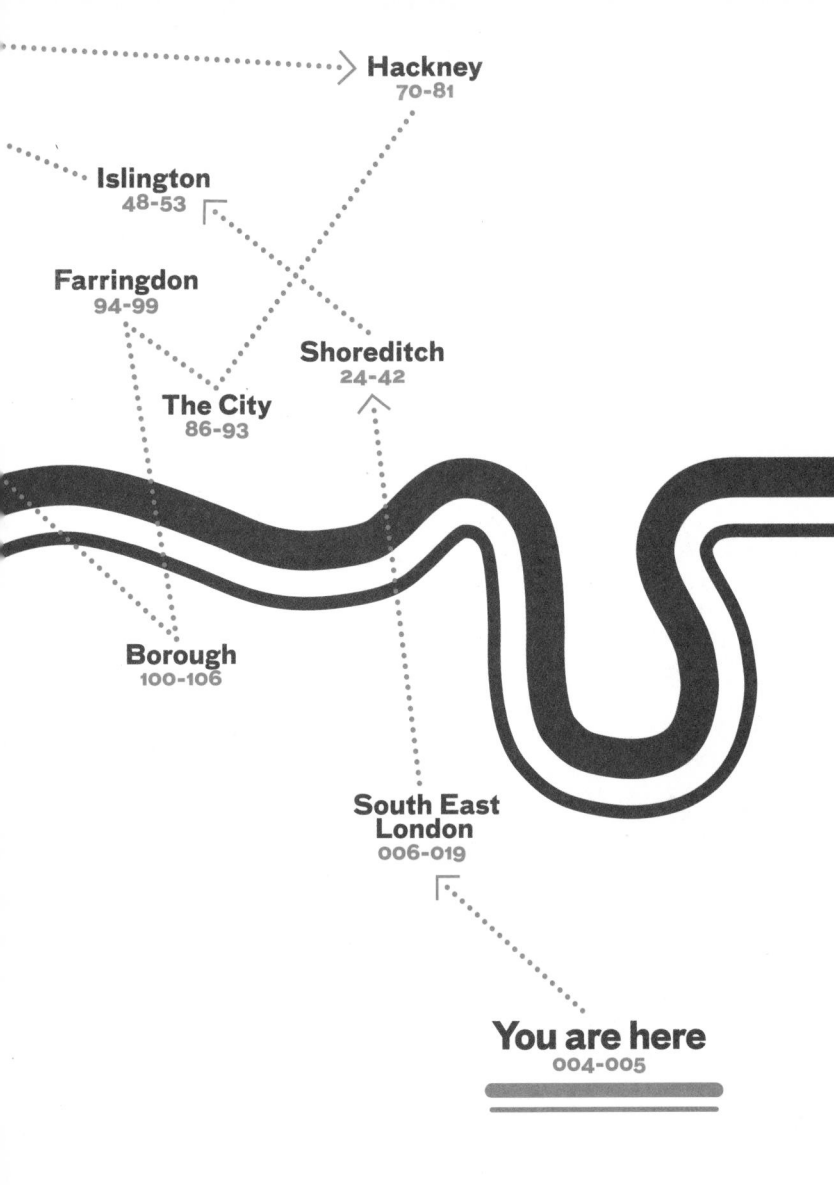

Tucked away in unfashionable South East London, New Cross had been touted as the 'New Shoreditch' for so many years now that you could be easily forgiven for feeling that the area would never fulfill its potential. The presence of Goldsmiths, one of the country's leading art and fashion colleges has meant that there was always a plentiful supply of questionably dressed students around and with them a fun if slightly ramshackle live scene, but few people would have considered a night out if they weren't locals.

All this changed though in 2007 when the people behind the Lock Tavern took over the dilapidated Amersham Arms and transformed it into one of London's best venues. New Cross was suddenly attracting artists like Hot Chip and with them a whole new crowd, most of whom had probably never ventured south of the river for a night out before. With nights covering everything from bleeding-edge electronica to hip-hop and indie and everyone from the freshest faced new rave band to rockney stalwarts Chas & Dave, The Arms has finally provided the area with a destination venue.

It's not all about one venue though and the Amersham Arms wouldn't exist without the work done by some of the area's less well-connected venues. Take a right at New Cross Gate station and you're a short walk from one of London's most eccentric pubs, the Montague Arms. While the pub's rundown exterior, dodgy location and incongruous sign claiming that tourists are welcome may be a little offputting, once in you'd be forgiven

Amersham Arms
388 New Cross Road
SE14 6TY
www.amersham-arms.co.uk

Montague Arms
289 Queens Rd
SE15 2PA

There's only so long that an area can remain up and coming before you start to get the feeling it's missed its chance.

for believing you'd fallen through the looking glass. From the menagerie's worth of stuffed animals, everything from zebra to mice, to the septugenarian bar staff oblivious to the throbbing electro-punk howl that can normally be heard coming from the stage, there's nothing normal about this pub.

Alternatively turn left out of the station, point your nose in the direction of the jerk chicken aromas and head up the high street to the New Cross Inn, a messy cross between a traditional-looking boozer and a Klaxons after party. The spiritual heart of the area's nightlife, it's like the Amersham Arms' younger brother and generally gives off the vibe that at any moment the pub's parents are going to get back off of holiday and chase all the brightly dressed ne'er-do-wells back to their grotty flats. It might not be the place to go for a sophisticated evening of cocktails but a night at the New Cross Inn is quite an experience and one that can end several days later.

Away from the booze and bands, SE14 might not be overflowing with options but there's still enough to fill a rainy day, Deptford Market is one the city's oldest, busiest and best markets, and the recently opened New Cross Gallery has already been home to several exhibitions of up-and-coming street artists. Gastronomically, the closest New Cross gets to fusion cuisine is a pizza with a kebab meat topping, but several of the pie shops in Deptford High Street are justly famous. Be warned though - the area hasn't completely lost its rough edges, the quality of live music and club nights in New Cross may be on the up and up, but the touts that await you at the station are probably more interested in relieving you of your old travelcards than your ticket to see Shitting Fists and the centre of New Cross is still dominated by The Venue, a five-story temple to bad music and sexually transmitted diseases that on any given night can resemble a cross between Fight Club and the last day of the TK Maxx sales. Still it's this clash of cultures that makes this often-ignored area one of London's most vibrant and creative and well worth risking a day and night away from some of London's more well-worn locales.

New Cross Gallery
3 Lewisham Way
SE14 6PP
www.gallery-london.co.uk

New Cross Inn
323 New Cross Road
SE14
www.myspace.com/
newcrossinn

Deptford Market
Deptford High Street
Weds, Fri, Sat

It's strange mix in Compendia. Old chaps in hats come in for bridge scorecards and those little pencils they like. Kids drop by to order lost pieces for their Pirates of the Caribbean board game. Landlords stock up on Double 6 Dominoes ('extra-thick tournament quality dominoes' at £14.95), and special three-player cribbage boards. It's also a bit of a Mecca for carrom fans – the shop's got lots of swish handmade tables for those of the finger-billiard persuasion.

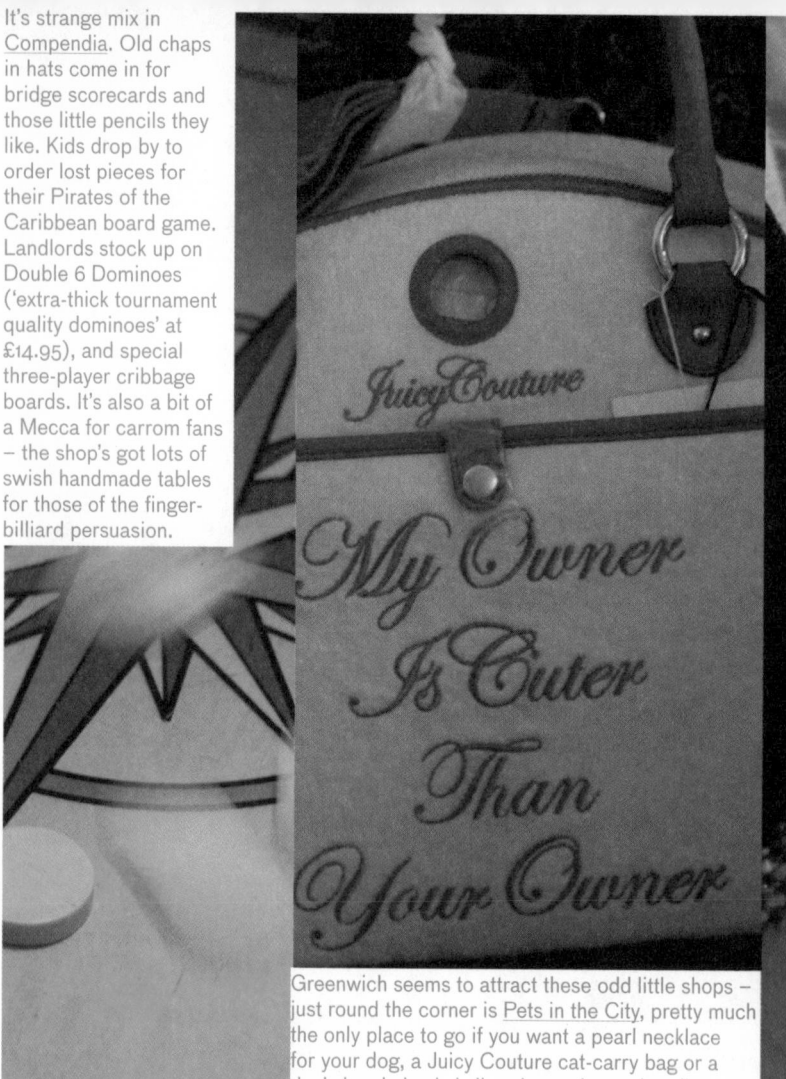

Greenwich seems to attract these odd little shops – just round the corner is Pets in the City, pretty much the only place to go if you want a pearl necklace for your dog, a Juicy Couture cat-carry bag or a dachshund-sized skull-and-crossbones hoodie.

Compendia
10, The Market,
SE10 9HZ, 11.00am -5.30pm
If you're there on a Saturday, check out the Tobiko market stall – fantastic fresh sushi rolled right in front of you.

Pets in the City
334 Creek Road
SE10 9SW
020 8858 3527

The Greenwich Dip

Seeing as we reward that proto-terrorist Guido Fawkes with a whole day of fireworks and baked potatoes, the least we can do for the hapless anarchist Martial Bourdin is to give him a LE COOL blue plaque. Bourdin was a French anarchist with a mission: to blow up Greenwich Observatory. Not for him an attack on the political or municipal systems of power, no, he was more audacious, he would take on the very highest symbols of time and geography themselves. Unfortunately his bomb-making skills were a little less rarefied than his rhetoric, and his device exploded prematurely. Locals will show you the various dips in the ground that are supposed to be Bourdin's final legacy. (Lovers of symmetry might like to take a trip straight from here to the 'Richmond Mound' a Bronze Age barrow pressed into use by Henry VIII for its uninterrupted view through to St Pauls where he could take a quick break from bothering the park's deer to check on the signals telling him whether his latest wife's beheading had gone ahead or not.)

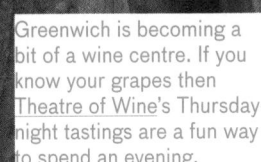

If you want to look a little more glamorous than Greenwich's dogs, root through some bling next door to Pets... among Emporium's piles of costume jewellery and fake fur.

Greenwich is becoming a bit of a wine centre. If you know your grapes then Theatre of Wine's Thursday-night tastings are a fun way to spend an evening.

Emporium
330-332 Creek Road
SE10 9SW

Theatre of Wine
75 Trafalgar Road
SE10 9TS020 8858 6363
www.theatreofwine.com
tastings@theatreofwine.com
email for places

Bar Du Musee
17 Nelson Road, SE10 9JB,
020 8858 4710. Only head out
to the back if you need a fag or
want to hear tourists discussing
the size of the Cutty Sark.

Tour guides don't usually take people to southeast London. St Pauls, yes. The East End maybe. But if you really want to delve a bit deeper into hidden London, you need someone like Kevin Caruth. His company Urban Gentry runs bespoke tours round stylish and secret London. We asked him for his favourite places in the southeast.

Forest Hill/Brockley

Horniman Museum

A jewel, set in gorgeous open grounds. An eclectic and extraordinary collection of natural history, culture and instruments (and an aquarium). The perfect place for a sunny afternoon.

100 London Road
SE23 3PQ
www.horniman.ac.uk

Id

An intimate store, with an ever-changing collection of 20th-century furniture and accessories, lovingly pulled together by the owner, George. Well worth a browse.

49 Honor Oak Park
SE23 1EA
www.idforlondon.com

Havelock Walk

A delightful cobbled mews in deepest southeast London. It's an energetic, buzzy enclave packed full of passionate folk, all committed to the creative cause. It's also filled with much-sought-after architect-designed houses and studios that hold regular open days.

Havelock Walk
SE23 3HG
www.havelockwalk.com/artists.html

The Rivoli Ballroom

One of London's few remaining ballrooms. A magnet for fans of vintage glamour, red velvet and glitter balls. Today, it plays host to ballroom dancers, film crews and quality cabaret.

350 Brockley Rd
SE4 2BY
www.therivoli.co.uk

Crystal Palace Park

A rugged, relatively un-manicured open park beloved by local residents. Highlights include a boating lake, the world's first life-size dinosaur replicas (now a bit dated), and London's largest maze. Take your time, there's a lot to see.

www.crystalpalacepark.net

This is Greenwich Village's massive showroom.

If you're in Greenwich Village then it's worth grabbing a cup of coffee at the café at the <u>Laban Centre</u> – turn right out of the estate and keep walking till the shabby industrial units give way to a sweeping glassy blade of a building. If there's a performance on, then you can catch the dance stars of tomorrow learning their craft. If not, they do a great cappuccino.

Only just opened to the public, it's a repository of pretty much everything cool that's happening in the furniture world. As you'd expect from guys who stared running bars and clubs, it's very classy, very friendly and very cool.

Unit C103
Faircharm Trading Estate
8 - 10 Creekside
SE8 3DX

Laban
Creekside
SE8 3DZ
020 8691 8600

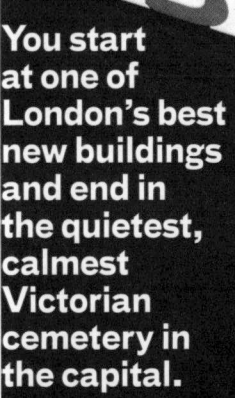

You start at one of London's best new buildings and end in the quietest, calmest Victorian cemetery in the capital.

Jump off

the bus at Peckham's glorious Will Alsop-designed library. There'll be hordes of tourists taking pictures outside, but it's really worth getting a pass to go inside. On a sunny day, the coloured panels of the cladding lend every room a different mood.

Peckham Library
122 Peckham Hill Street
SE15 5JR
020 7525 2000

Then turn right

down the high street and pop in to say hi to Sally Butcher in <u>Persepolis</u> at number 28. Not just a one-stop shop for all things Persian, this is also where chefs at London's best Middle Eastern restaurants come for their ingredients.

Persepolis
28-30 Peckham High Street
SE15 5DT
020 7639 8007

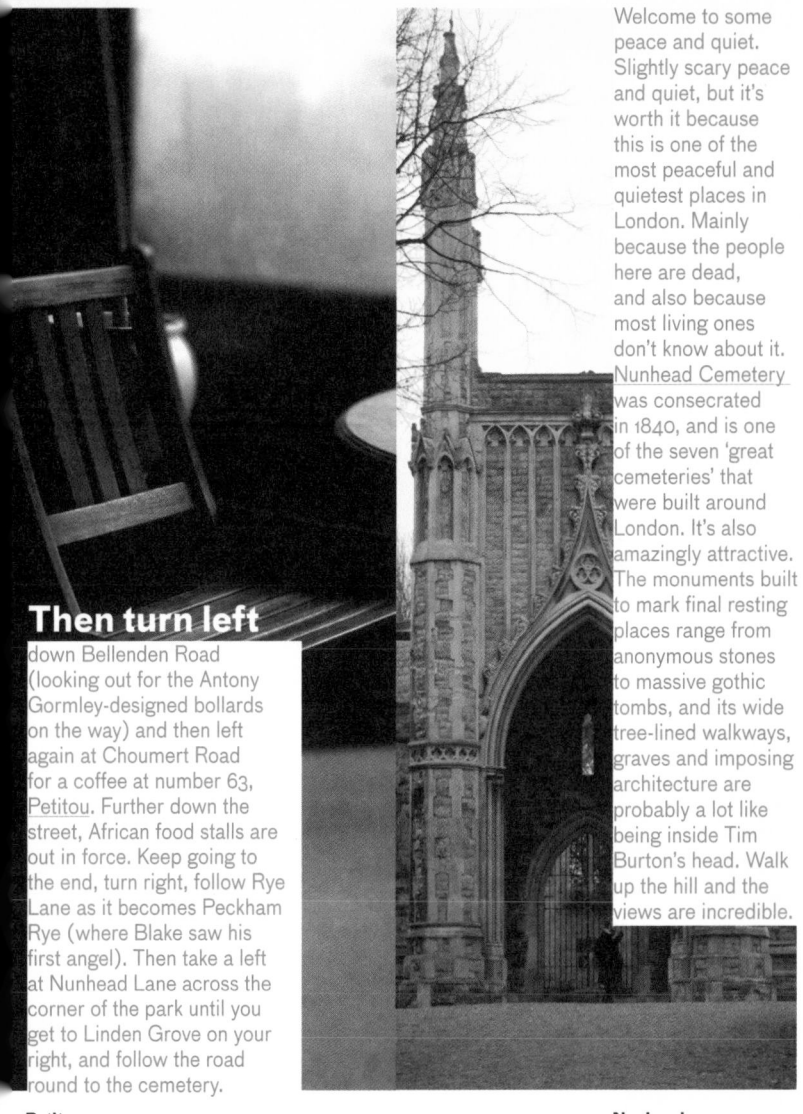

Welcome to some peace and quiet. Slightly scary peace and quiet, but it's worth it because this is one of the most peaceful and quietest places in London. Mainly because the people here are dead, and also because most living ones don't know about it. Nunhead Cemetery was consecrated in 1840, and is one of the seven 'great cemeteries' that were built around London. It's also amazingly attractive. The monuments built to mark final resting places range from anonymous stones to massive gothic tombs, and its wide tree-lined walkways, graves and imposing architecture are probably a lot like being inside Tim Burton's head. Walk up the hill and the views are incredible.

Then turn left

down Bellenden Road (looking out for the Antony Gormley-designed bollards on the way) and then left again at Choumert Road for a coffee at number 63, Petitou. Further down the street, African food stalls are out in force. Keep going to the end, turn right, follow Rye Lane as it becomes Peckham Rye (where Blake saw his first angel). Then take a left at Nunhead Lane across the corner of the park until you get to Linden Grove on your right, and follow the road round to the cemetery.

Petitou
63 Choumert Road
SE15 4AR
020 7639 2613

Nunhead Cemetery
Linden Grove
SE15 3LF
020 7732 9535

The master confectioner, Hope & Greenwood claims that Willy Wonka keeps a 'close eye' on the place though in fact he's more likely to be quaking in his boots. On your first visit, it's hard not to go all Augustus Gloop, trying to sample every truffle, bonbon and toffee in reach. The shop's heady blend of 1950s-style presentation conjures up a pre-Twix era, with chocs nestled in silver trays on dark wood, rows of old-fashioned glass sweet jars and amiable staff. Husband-and-wife team Mr Greenwood and Miss Hope search out the best handmade sweets in the country, as well as Fairtrade chocolate and even sweet tobacco. Delicious ice cream in the summer and their famous Christmas window in winter keep kids – including big ones – flocking there all year round.

Chener Books is for those who mourn the closing of old-school, independent bookshops. According to owner John Kennedy, a secondhand-book shop stood on the site some thirty years ago, pre-dating gentrified East Dulwich. His place mainly stocks new books, however, boasting impressive Wordsworth Classics, specialist music and travel sections. Each week, they raid the secondhand section for their window display, and on our visit, we coveted several collectors' annuals all dating from the most literary of years, 1984.

Hope & Greenwood
20 Northcross Road
SE22 9EU
0870 850 9049
www.hopeandgreenwood.co.uk

Chener Books
14 Lordship Lane
SE22 8HN
020 8299 0771

The good news is that Thai Corner Café, possibly London's tiniest neighbourhood restaurant, doesn't have room for E Dul's ubiquitous jumbo buggies.

This jewel on Northcross Street has been dishing out cheap and tasty Bangkok fare for ten years, with attentive yet unobtrusive service in a setting so relaxed, it feels like you've gatecrashed someone's home. Starters include fish cakes, tom yum soup and vegetarian tung tong (dumplings with tofu). Main dishes are served to spec (die-hard vegetarians can avoid the oyster or shrimp sauce), and include Thai curries and stir-fries, with the priciest dish still under £8. Their BYOB is another excuse to visit, with bottle corkage at £2 for wine or 50p for beer.

Thai Corner Café
44 North Cross Road
SE22 9EU
020 8299 4041

A slice of the Big Apple is served up on Lordship Lane in the shape of <u>Inside 72</u>. The décor features half-plastered walls, a Billie Holliday print, a collection of toy robots and a horned cow skull. During the day, plonk yourself on a leather sofa and take in the foot traffic outside through the full-length windows. At night an arty, unpretentious crowd enjoys a soundtrack ranging from Blondie to the Yeah Yeah Yeahs, with bottled-beer options featuring Brooklyn lager. With low-hanging bulbs and a neon sign illuminating a cute little disco ball, you could easily imagine yourself in the heart of the East Village.

<u>Black Cherry</u> is an apt venue for a Woody Allen-esque double date, where your partner and 'the perfect couple' can sit for hours and ruminate over Fellini's finer points, à la *Manhattan*. This family-run place morphs between a restaurant, a café and a cocktail bar, and though a recent addition to 'the strip', it is already an institution. The décor boasts avocado wallpaper in Venetian-style print, gilded mirrors, dark wooden tables and giant bejeweled light shades. Grab a coffee and share an apple tart tartin – a true slice of heaven. Alternatively, a dinner of Spanish frittata with salad followed by spicy seafood linguine here won't break the bank. For cocktails, we say try a Gingita (ginger-infused gin, passion fruit purée with a dash of lemon) or a Black Cherry Alexander (Courvoisier VS Cognac, crème de cerise and black cherry ice cream dusted with shavings of Hope & Greenwood organic chocolate).

Inside 72
72 Lordship Lane
SE22 8HF
020 8693 7131

Black Cherry
21 Lordship Lane
SE22 8EW
020 8299 8877
www.blackcherrybar.co.uk

MARKET SPECIALS

Sardines w/salad
bread, fresh chilli £5
& garlic dressing.
Tilapia w/salad £ 7/9
and salsa sauce.

£4

We're all guilty of it – swinging out of pub doors saloon-style, our feet and stomach together herding us as fast as possible to the nearest chippy. Fortunately, the Sea Cow is no standard, greasy fish bar. Taking its cue from eateries down under, the experience is immediately arresting. Firstly, the whole place is spotless with an uber-modern stainless steel counter. There are at least five uniformed servers, who greet you promptly and in a friendly manner. The fish is laid out on display, all sourced and delivered daily from the coast or from Billingsgate Fish Market. Fish can be cooked to your specifications – grilled, poached, and so on – and the chips are fat and succulent without being oily. Inventive daily market specials appear on the board: sardines with salad; bread, fresh chilli and garlic dressing, tilapia fish with salad and salsa. The dining area also breaks the takeaway rules – it has clean, chunky wooden tables with enough space to swing a hungry cat. The Sea Cow doubles as a fishmonger, and you can order items in advance. Leave the pub early - just this once, your feet and stomach are right.

Sea Cow
37 Lordship Lane
SE22 8EW
020 8693 3111
www.theseacow.co.uk
12pm-11pm Tue-Sat, 12pm-8.30pm Sun

The website doesn't deal in anything as mundane as an address or a phone number. It almost like the <u>Wapping Project</u> don't want you to find them. Which would be a shame because it's a fantastic gallery. Like a baby Tate Modern, it's set in an old industrial space, but unlike its big sister, it's still crammed with machinery, and every inch of the space has been used. On a recent visit, the roof had been flooded and a small boat was moored overlooking the Thames as the shipping forecast played mournfully from speakers. Downstairs in the boiler house, an entire forest had been recreated and towering trees scraped the beams of the ceiling. The turbine hall's restaurant was busy with visitors eating dinner in the light of candles dotted over the old machines, and even the trees outside were festooned with hundreds of yellow silk umbrellas.

It doesn't show up on cabbies' sat-nav.

The Wapping Project
Wapping Hydraulic Power Station
Wapping Wall
E1W 3SGW
www.thewappingproject.com

Wilton's Music Hall

It was the meeting place for the anti-fascists before the Battle of Cable Street. The first ever can-can was performed here. And then banned. It's the default backdrop for rock photographers who want to show that a band has a bit of depth and history. Y'know, like Muse or someone. It's the world's oldest music hall. It served 2000 meals a day to striking dockers in 1889. It's the "handsomest room in town". (It's not strictly speaking open to the public, except for special events. But drop them an email. They're really nice).

Graces Alley
Off Ensign Street
London E1 8JB

www.wiltons.org.uk

Across the road is London's oldest riverside pub. It has two very different literary claims to fame: Pepys drank here while on naval business in Wapping, and it was the post-work pub of choice for Sun journalists when they used to be down the road. It's full of tourist trade nowadays – a far cry from the bare-knuckle boxers and cock fighters who once frequented the place – but it's still a good place to sit on the balcony and watch the sun set over the river.

The Prospect of Whitby
57 Wapping Wall
E1W 3SJ

Head to the ends of the tube and there are strange pleasures to be found. The stretch east from the scruffy back windows of Leyton out through the fields and meadows of Essex to Epping. Or sitting at the front of a DLR train, pretending to be the driver as you swoop between back gardens to Canary Wharf.

But, but, but... a total guilty pleasure is getting a black cab, 2am, and just driving back and forth over the Thames bridges. The heater on, Magic playing softly from the front, a head on your shoulder and lights on the water...

Tubes vs Taxis

Dukes Hotel
St James's Place
SW1A 1NY
020 7491 4840

Teas vs Torture

Time to get all dressed up.

If it's the suit or flowery blouse look that you're rocking, then the best afternoon tea in town is in the Victorian conservatory at Dukes.

But if there's anything more British than afternoon tea then it's a spot of light bondage. Dust off your gimp mask for the Torture Garden parties. It's a Bank Holiday tradition.

Torture Garden
www.torturegarden.com

SHOREDITCH

This is the size of a garage – I'm warning you, it ain't big. But <u>Casita</u> is run by a very friendly man called Will, and he prides himself on serving authentic South American beers and cocktails. He's also next in line to be an Earl, and it's not every day you get served by actual British aristocracy.

The barmen are more bothered about getting you exactly what you want than rushing on to the next person, the drinks are freshly made in front of you with a bit of friendly banter, and they're not pre-mixed dishwater. Plus, the music's pretty good too. Just remember to turn the toilet light out when you're done in there – it saves on the leccy you see...

Check out the mojitos and Casita-style tequila shots.

Casita
5 Ravey St
EC2A 4QW
www.myspace.com/casitabar

When we went to take pictures of NOG, Max the owner said he didn't want to be in any guidebook, he didn't need it. He wouldn't relent till I'd told him the last thing I'd bought at NOG. Luckily he approved. And then he invited us to an unadvertised gig by Jackie O Motherfucker in the basement – it's that kind of place.)

It's been fun watching the rise of <u>NOG</u>.

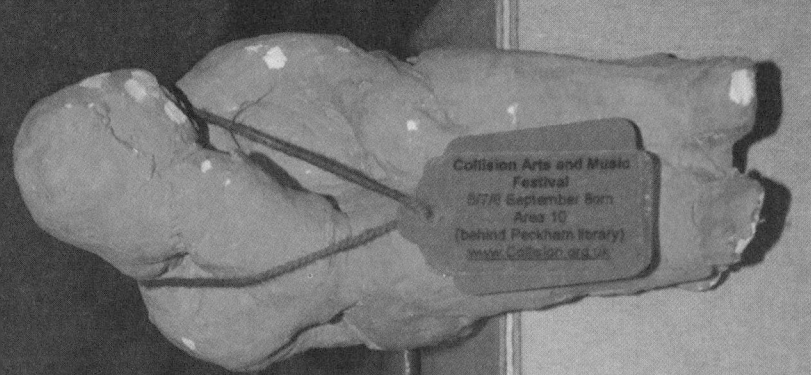

It started as the new kid on the block, a tiny illustration gallery on a street where galleries are ten-a-penny. Then it started stocking cool art books and hard-to-find magazines for the cognoscenti who gathered there. Once they admitted to themselves that they'd turned into a fully fledged hang-out, they added a bar and coffee shop. The most recent additions are a record shop (though there's a sneaking suspicion these LPs might have been chosen purely for their covers) and a tiny gig-space downstairs where oh-so-cool secret gigs are held.

Despite the distractions, NOG remains the champion of handmade, hand-drawn art. The walls are covered with fantastic work torn from notebooks, the shelves are full of tiny one-person fanzines. You'll find tiny doodles next to intricate sprawling monstrosities. Works by unknown students sit next to Kim Gordon's drawings. What you won't find is anything dull, or mass-produced or empty. Long live NOG.

Nog
182 Brick Lane
E1 6SA
020 7739 4134
www.noggallery.com

You don't visit <u>Dennis Severs'</u> <u>House</u> so much as sneak around it. A loving facsimile of an 18th- and 19th-century home, it's like an especially adult haunted house. The jumbled domestic rooms appear very recently vacated - smells of freshly-peeled oranges and hot coffee waft over half-eaten meals and scattered papers, and the beds are rumpled in a way that convinces you they're still warm. Dennis himself passed away in 1999, and he left behind not only the rooms but also tiny messages in each one, pointing out his favourite details. Monday evenings you can skulk about silently by candlelight, and with very little effort mess quite splendidly with your own head.

Dennis Severs House
18 Folgate Street
Spitalfields
E1 6BX
www.dennissevershouse.co.uk

True story

I used to work on Brick Lane. In my lunch breaks, I used to wander around the area, and would often pass a little door marked "FUTURIST FOOD – EVENTS HERE AND ELSEWHERE OCCASIONALLY"

It was always closed.

Then, one winter's evening, I was heading home and saw a light on behind the door. So I knocked. Inside was Giles Prince, castle-builder, filmmaker and Futurist food guru.

He invited me to one of his legendary dinner parties. Futurist food, it turns out, is experimental dining, where the idea is more important than the taste.

Giles has made banquets for Christie's Italian art sales, featuring metre-long jellies containing fibre optics and houses made of chocolate that you eat with tiny hammers. At the party I attended, we ate snails in go-faster sauce. We ate carp carpaccio, we ate crenellations of quince in cardboard castles. It was good. Someone broke a £15,000 mirror.

If you want a castle built, or to eat some genuinely original food, Giles is your man. He asked us not to print his address, but there are enough clues here, if you really want to find him. Just hope he's in.

A wintery Thursday night. Wandering home from photographing the Bodhi Gallery (three pages on). Soft clouds of white breath rise from a crowd outside Corbet Place.

Inside is Brazilian music, couples spinning, sweating and spinning. Outside is cigarettes and soft conversation. Lean in, take a couple of quick pictures. No one stops – everyone's lost to the music.

"Hey, what is this place?"

"Forro do Galpao"
Free, Thursdays
Corbet Place
The Old Truman Brewery
15 Hanbury Street
E1 6QR

'I've heard wonderful things about your food.'

'Oh yeah? Did you hear about the mad lady who runs it?'

'Yes I did.'

'That's me.'

Oops.

'They came to take me away in a white van,' laughs the renowned mad lady of Lennie's. She's joking of course... or is she? An innocuous-enough Shoreditch sandwich joint by day, this duplicitous nook on Calvert Avenue transforms into a cheap and delicious Thai eatery by night. It's a fairly tatty interior, and service is impeccably brusque. If there's time, the mickey-taking, faux-stern owner will give a run-down of the dishes and make recommendations, but it's simple really: get the fish. For large groups, call in advance to say how many hungry people will be turning up, and they'll lay on a set feast that'll have you stuffed to maximum capacity.

Lennie's (dinner)
6 Calvert Avenue
E2 7JP
020 7739 3628

Pay attention cos this one's hard to find.

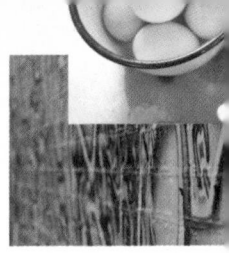

Nominally a grocer's, but in reality the de facto Shoreditch artists' breakfast hangout, Leila's has a fairly short menu.

1) Eggs. With Serrano ham or sage.
2) Toast. With whatever.

It's pretty much all you need. Squeeze in along the one battered table by the kitchen and wait for someone to wash up some cutlery for you. The eggs come fried and dripping in butter, served still in the pan (saves on washing up). Watch the Shoreditch art world shake off its hangover and decide to go and get a pint of milk, eavesdrop on who did what to who at Suzie's opening last night, and pick up fresh supplies for a London Fields picnic.

(Top tip. Combining 1) and 2) above makes for just about the best fried egg sandwich in the world.)

Probably the best way to find the Rochelle School Canteen is to follow a hungry-looking artist. Find Arnold Circus (you can't miss it - it contains the only living grass for about ten miles). Walk anti-clockwise till you see the Rochelle School artists' studios. (Harder than you'd think - there are four sets of studios on the circus. Rochelle is the one that looks nothing like studios.) Check the buzzers for CANTEEN. Buzz. Wait. Wait some more. If no one lets you in, wait for a starving artist to open the door for you.

It's worth the effort. In the former school's bikeshed is an amazing canteen run by Nose To Tail Eating, the art world's caterers of choice who are based in the same building. That means unlikely canteen fare like lamb neck and smoked eel and horseradish. It means really decent coffee. And it means you can bring your own booze.

Leila's (breakfast)
17 Calvert Avenue
E2 7JP
020 7729 9789

Rochelle School (lunch)
Arnold Circus
E2 7ES
020 7729 5677
info@nosetotail.com
www.afoundation.org.uk/rochelle/index.php

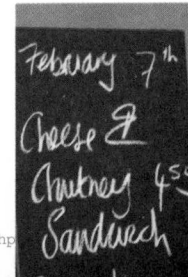

February 7th
Cheese &
Chutney 4.50
Sandwich

In a basement under Brick Lane there's a bunch of Japanese kids silently reading the latest instalment of Ghost In The Shell and drinking green tea. Upstairs there's art on the walls - Farris Rotter and Jaime Dechanel have showed here - but downstairs is where it's at - the UK's first manga library. In Japan these places crop up everywhere but east Londoners are getting used to the idea of paying a pound an hour to catch up on the weekly tales. A great place to recharge your batteries before risking the crowds of Brick Lane again.

Bodhi Gallery
214 Brick Lane
E1 6SA
020 7749 0750

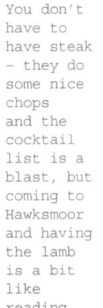

You don't have to have steak - they do some nice chops and the cocktail list is a blast, but coming to Hawksmoor and having the lamb is a bit like reading Penthouse for the articles.

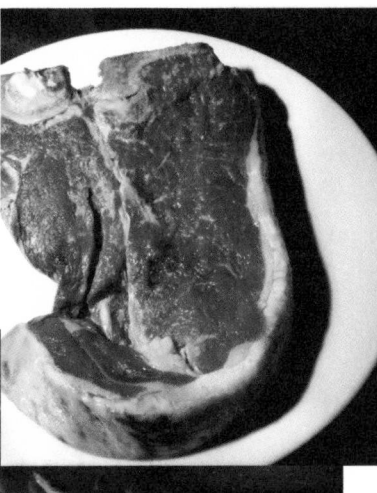

"Ladies and gentlemen, weighing in at 600 grams, lovingly reared in Yorkshire by the Ginger Pig butchers, hung for 28 days then cooked on a charcoal grill, I give you…
drum roll…
the Hawksmoor steak."

Hawksmoor
157 Commercial Street
E1 6BJ
0207 247 7392

Atmospheric film boutique WLTM Shoreditch cinema geeks for fun times, romance and the occasional classic horror. From the cult to the corny, Today is Boring offers an old-world rental service for the download generation, by way of a meticulously amassed pile of catalogues. No timewasters, please.

Today Is Boring
15 Kingsland Road
E2 8AA
020 7684 1461
www.todayisboring.com
Daily 2pm - 10pm

An epicurean jewel set on Hoxton's least gentrifiable street. This converted Victorian boozer sees experimental head chef Nuno Mendes serve up dishes of red mullet with liquorice toast and 24-hour cooked pork jowl with langoustine, leek and nashi pear.

This self-proclaimed 'no-bullshit hotel' is a slice of the Big Apple, slap bang in Shoreditch's party Mecca. The lobby's exposed brickwork lends it an industrial feel and staff are always cool and collected. The rooms are paired-down – stylish yet functional with flat-screen TVs,

free water and wifi. Bathrooms are uber-cool with excellent power showers and the comfy bed means you'll sleep like a baby. Here you can reap the benefits of a high-end hotel but at a fraction of the price. A hands-down obvious choice for the NME awards post-party.

Bacchus
177 Hoxton Street
N1 6PJ
020 7613 0477
www.bacchus-restaurant.co.uk

Hoxton Hotel
81 Great Eastern Street
EC2A 3HU
020 7550 1000

Wood-lined corridors lead away under huge creaking chandeliers to shadowy rooms with 12-foot fireplaces on every wall. Your eyes follow acres of medieval friezes and vast statues up to the vaulted ceiling. This is where you go if you want to buy a 19th-century gentleman's library, or a Gothic-Revival oak pedestal with an arched Neo-Gothic cornice. Or if you just want to feel like you've drunk the shrinking potion from Alice in Wonderland.

Westland
Church of St Michael and All Angels
Mark Street (off Paul Street)
EC2A 4ER
020 7739 0448

This little cornershop has many guises, from slightly hidden secondhand wedding-dress emporium, to art gallery, jewellery store, skull purveyor and ceramics exhibitor. Luna & Curious is what happens when eight artists get together and create a shrine to surreal romance. Two of their best ideas so far are the feathering service and the T Shirt Patisserie. With the first, you bring in your tired and poor soles and £100 later, a true Cinderella is returned to you, covered in feathers of your choice. The T Shirt Patisserie, on the other hand, offers you the possibility of the creating a unique wearable present, including pretty, pretty wrapping paper and a sweet bonus. How curious.

Luna & Curious
198 Brick Lane
E1
020 8981 1655
www.lunaandcurious.com
www.tshirtpatisserie.com

To say the staff are friendly is a massive understatement. If owner Neil isn't personally pulling pints then it's his brother, flatmate, girlfriend, etc. Sure, it's a little grimy, but doesn't idly swatting away barflies from your drink add to the romance? Everything about it is timeless, except for the changed-every-so-often art on the walls, and the tags in the toilets. One of our favourite things about Indo is its positively Irish attitude towards trading hours; the staff seeming genuinely disappointed when you finally tag-out, get them to de-bar the doors and leave the party.

Get there early, bag yourself the Chesterfield in time for sundown, and snuggle in for the long haul.

INDO
133 Whitechapel Road
E1 1DT
Brick Lane
020 7247 4926
Noon-1am Mon-Thur
Sun; noon-3am Fri, Sat
Food served noon-3pm, 6-9pm daily

It's 3.15am, you're on your way home and hungry. You're about to confront the issue that truly divides Londoners.

Not Labour vs Tory.
Not north vs south.
Not Arsenal vs Chelsea.

Which of the two 24-hour bagel shops at the top of Brick Lane do you go to?

On the left they make 'em fresh in front of you. And they do a good jam tart.

On the right is the original – loyal genuine eastenders tend to eat here. And the salt beef is better.

Whichever you choose, we give a silent cheer for London's cheapest, friendliest all-night food shops.

Brick Lane Beigel Bake
159 Brick Lane
E1 6SB
0871 332 8040

Beigel Shop
155 Brick Lane
E1 6SB
020 7729 0826

sh!

Sh! is a sex shop for women, filled with female erotica in predictably pretty packaging. Expect an onslaught of pink, an affable welcome, a library of niche literature and a range of wares, from an innocuous slip of flirty underwear to full-blown bedroom artillery. Enjoy it girls, there isn't a trench-coated man in sight.

Sh!
57 Hoxton Square
N1
020 7613 5458
Open daily 12pm-8pm
www.sh-womenstore.com
Men must be
accompanied by women

THE FRENZ EXPERIMENT

THE WONDERFUL AND FRIGHTEN-ING WORLD OF... THE FALL

PERVERTED BY LANGUAGE

SEMINAL LIVE

THE LIGHT USER SYNDROME

BEND SINISTER

I AM KURIOUS ORANJ

THIS NATION'S SAVING GRACE
LAY OF THE LAND

As guitarist with The Fall, Brix Smith played on some of the bolshiest, most raucous, in fact some of the best records ever made by human beings. She wrote Hey! Luciani, spiked the Fall's Mancunian dourness with a dollop of Californian psychedelia, and generally swanned around looking like the coolest thing ever to strap on a vintage Rickenbacker.

That'd be enough for 'Legend' status, but her second career is just as cool. Finding there was 'nowhere to shop' when she moved out to Shoreditch in 2000, she went ahead and opened up the boutique Start. It pulls off the same trick as she did in The Fall – taking a grim and grey British institution and filling it with a playful glitz and glamour.

Start
42-44 Rivington Street
EC2A 3BN
020 7729 3334
Mon-Fri, 10.30am-6.30pm
Sat, 11am-6.30pm, Sun, 1pm-6pm

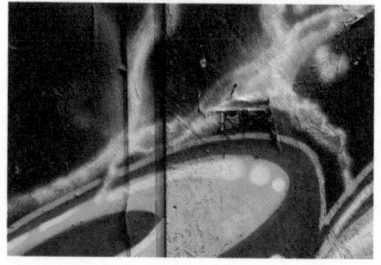

Art galleries, strip club, lounge
Street has everything you'd want on

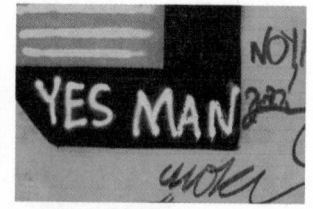

Strip Club

The White Horse
64 Shoreditch High Street
E1 6JJ
020 7739 3702

Art Galleries

Museum 52
52 Redchurch Street
E2 7DP
020 7366 5571

Studio 1.1
57a Redchurch Street
E2 7DJ

Vegas Gallery
64-66 Redchurch Street
E2 7DP
020 7729 4819

Trolley Gallery
73a Redchurch Street
E2 7DJ
020 7729 6591

bars, furniture shops. Redchurch
a Sunday (but where's the church?)

Bars

Owl and the Pussycat
34 Redchurch Street
E2 7DP
020 7613 3628

Lounge Lover
1 Whitby Street
E2 7DP
020 7012 1234

Furniture shops

Squint
3 Redchurch Street
E2 7DJ
020 7739 9275

Saffire
52 Redchurch Street
E2 7DP
020 7729 5205

They filter and bottle tap water on site.

The food's ethical, local and organic. Cooling from the canal, heating from solar panels.

(So, you expect it's going to all be a bit worthy but hey, you should support them anyway.

And you go and it turns out that the food is the best part of the whole thing – fabulous, flavoursome modern British cooking in a smart canalside dining room – and you think 'this might just be the future.')

Owned by a charity, the restaurant's profits go back into the community. Wormeries and composters make sure nothing's wasted. All the cooking is powered by hydro-electricity.

Water House
10 Orsman Road
N1 5QJ
020 7033 0123

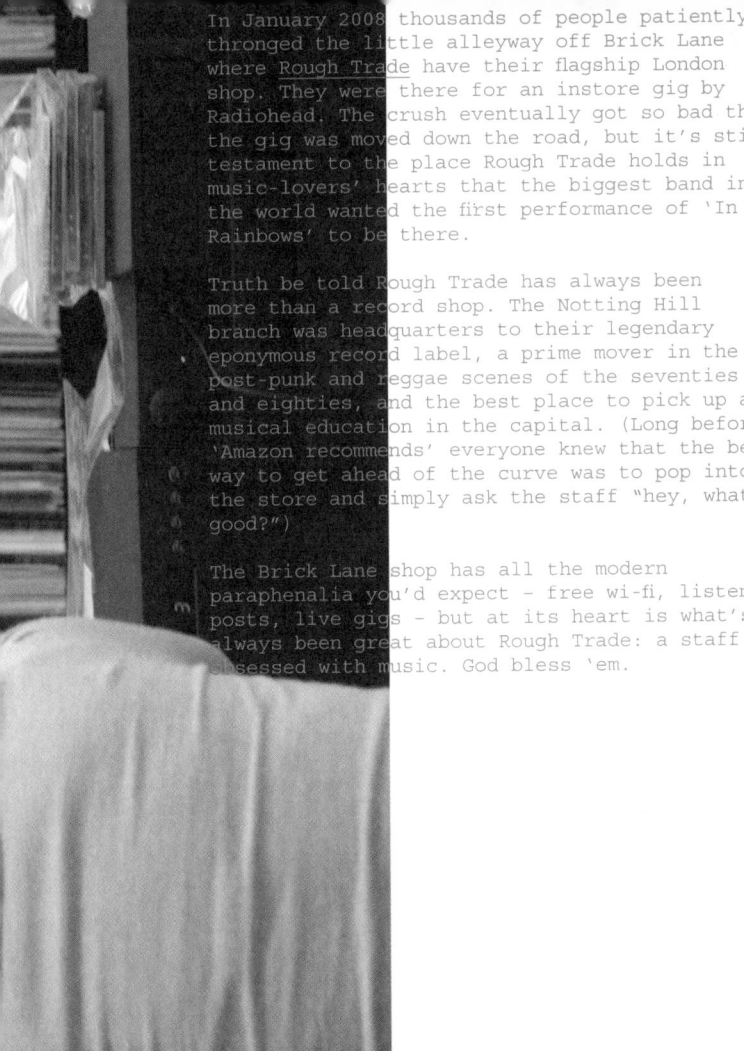

In January 2008 thousands of people patiently thronged the little alleyway off Brick Lane where Rough Trade have their flagship London shop. They were there for an instore gig by Radiohead. The crush eventually got so bad that the gig was moved down the road, but it's still testament to the place Rough Trade holds in music-lovers' hearts that the biggest band in the world wanted the first performance of 'In Rainbows' to be there.

Truth be told Rough Trade has always been more than a record shop. The Notting Hill branch was headquarters to their legendary eponymous record label, a prime mover in the post-punk and reggae scenes of the seventies and eighties, and the best place to pick up a musical education in the capital. (Long before 'Amazon recommends' everyone knew that the best way to get ahead of the curve was to pop into the store and simply ask the staff "hey, what's good?")

The Brick Lane shop has all the modern paraphenalia you'd expect – free wi-fi, listening posts, live gigs – but at its heart is what's always been great about Rough Trade: a staff obsessed with music. God bless 'em.

Rough Trade East
Dray Walk, Old Truman Brewery
91 Brick Lane
E1 6QL
020 7392 7788

PPPPRRRRAAAARRRRRPPPP!!!!!

The klaxon sounds and all hell breaks loose.

Six-foot-something guys are pulling off pink tutus and begging nearby girls for their skirts.

A petite lass in a boiler suit is slipping into a cardigan that reaches her knees.

And someone's asking me for my trousers.

The idea behind Swaparama Razzmatazz is simple. Play cheesy crowd-pleasers, make sure everyone's had a drink or two and then get them swapping clothes when the klaxon sounds. Part secondhand shop, part nightclub and a testament to how little it takes to get your average Englishman into a skirt, this is London's greatest ice-breaker.

Swaparama Razzmatazz
Favela Chic
91-93 Great Eastern Street EC2
020 7613 5228
www.myspace.com/swaparamarazzmatazz

Upset The Rhythm's Top 5 underground DIY venues

All smiles and glistening sweat, Upset The Rhythm know how to throw a party. The underground promoters and record label are the pumping heart of the city's DIY music scene throwing gigs for the most exciting new bands in the world – in equally inspiring venues. It all started in December 2003 with Deerhhoof in basement of an Italian wine bar called Needles – played through a glorified bass amp. Since then the crew have rolled out, big time. Chris Tipton, Claire Titley, Luke Nava, Chukka, Tanith Davidson, Aymie Backler and Dan Bolger have collectively thrown over 100 shows with dynamite bands such as No Age, Mika Miko, Brother Reade and Dan Deacon marking their UK debut performances by breaking hearts and stomping feet at UTR.

www.upsettherhythm.co.uk

1
Barden's Boudoir
38-40 Stoke Newington Road
N16 7XJ
020 7249 9557
www.bardensbar.co.uk
280 cp

"At a Gang Gang Dance show a friend told us they were going to open up the basement of an abandoned furniture shop and coincidently two of Upset The Rhythm lived directly behind. Our first show at Barden's was their first too – Lightning Bolt in 2004 and 600 people turned up. When Lightning Bolt were soundchecking they were still building and varnishing the bar. Part of the excitement was that nobody knew how and where the bands were going to set up. UTR's Chukka crowd-surfed with a video camera most of that night. It's an outsider space and we saw the potential. I doubt there would be a venue there if we hadn't done that one show. It put both us and Barden's on the map."

2
Café Oto
18-22 Ashwin St
Print House
E8 3DL
200 cp

"This is a newer space slightly further down the road from Barden's, directly behind the McDonalds opposite Dalston Kingsland station. We checked it out a couple of months before it opened and it's awesome. It's the ground floor of a printworks, and Hackney Council helped set it up as a space for a lot of the jazz guys from the area. This is a space that we're really excited about because after the Red Rose closed (one of the more important underground venues in London), this is amazing for hosting events on a shoestring budget. It's a really cool, barren gallery space, with a café in the day and shows in the evening. It's very much an Upset The Rhythm venue of the future."

3
Gramaphone
60-62 Commercial Street
E1 6LT
020 7377 5332
www.thegramaphone.co.uk
175 cp (100 comfortably)

"Gramaphone is an odd fish. In 2006 we were looking for a place to throw a noise show and it came to us more out of necessity. It's become quite a subversive grotto-like venue. Over the past year a lot more interesting events have been thrown here, which is inspiring, and it's usually available if you're a first-time promoter looking for a venue. They don't come more sincere than Gramaphone, there are no pretensions here – just great sound, a super atmosphere and you can't help but get involved. It's almost a homage to one of our favourite venues of yore – the Arts Café, which was a block further down and had some great shows from guys like Animal Collective."

4
Jamboree
566 Cable Street
E1W 3HB
200 cp

"This is another new space that we think is going to be really important. Our friend Simon was doing a lot of parties in his house and he got together with this guy Alistair and they both now own a warehouse space right next door to Limehouse station. It's a pretty basic PA and the stage at the moment is just some crates with wooden planks, but I know it will be a hub for underground music in London. It's free to use and has a license until 4am every day of the week, it's really cool - very much like a New York loft space."

5
Corsica Studios
Units 4/5, Elephant Road
SE17 1LB
020 7703 4760
www.corsicastudios.com
500 cp

"Over the last few years Corsica's established itself as a very important space for experimental music. Two of Upset The Rhythm proposed to each other there! We curated a party there using the two basic warehouse rooms under the railway arches, with six bands including Yellow Swans, Arrington De Dionyso and Astral Social Scene. There is a lot of electronic experimental music as well as performance art. Sometimes they use the front of house as a gallery – it's a really versatile space. The people who run it are great and are always open to new ideas."

THE WESTBOURNE HAS BECOME A MECCA OF GRAFFITI IN THE 80's AND 90's. HEADS WOULD TRAVEL FROM FAR AND WIDE TO SEE BURNERS BY NON STOP ART-JUSTICE AND RICH AND RAGE. IT'S STILL A HOTSPOT TODAY AND ARGUABLY IT'S GETTING HARDER TO CATCH THE REAL BURNERS UP IN THERE. LOOK OUT FOR SKORE, SHINE AND THE ODD FOREIGN BURNER

SOUTH BANK IS ANOTHER CLASSIC SPOT. IT'S HARD TO LIST THE ARTISTS THAT HAVE PAINTED THERE. (BUT IN THE PAST FEW YEARS, I HAVE INCLUDED—THIRD DEGREE CREW, ELSEONE AND BANZAI, PLUS LOADS OF FOREIGN HEADS PASSING THROUGH.) ONE MAINLY TO THE SHORT SHELF LIFE OF PAINTINGS THERE. THEY GET REPAINTED BY ARTISTS SUPER QUICK. FACT OF PAINTING DOWN AT SOUTH BANK IS UNDERSTANDING HOW DISPOSABLE THIS PROBLEM CAN BE. BUT YOUR WORK CAN EXPECT AN AUDIENCE OF UP TO 100,000 PEOPLE A DAY!

Sunday Clubbing

Located within sinfully convenient stumbling distance of each other, Shoreditch's Sunday clubs have teased out the concept of the afterparty to create 24 hours of Sabbath-day debauchery for the most committed of London's party people. This dedicated crowd worships at the altar of disco, and lo, they maketh their midday pilgrimage East to share a podium rather than a pew. Sunday clubbing diva Sophie Walker is your guide.

12pm
Kubicle at Public Life. This converted public toilet is an erm, intimate venue, irreverently located in the shadow of the glacial Hawksmoor church that dominates Spitalfields market. Kubicle regulars Freak 'n' Chic and Hector dish out deep house and techno to a grateful, glamorous, multicoloured crowd, mostly wearing statement sunglasses to shade their blown-out retinas from the daylight filtering through the glass bricks in the ceiling. This is the place to spot chomping, bedraggled but seriously determined folks on the back-end of an all-nighter, rubbing up against perfectly preened Sunday scene aficionados who are just starting the biggest party of their weekend.

3:30pm
Trip up Brick Lane and dodge the lightweights nursing yesterday's hangover with pints outside the Truman Brewery. This could be the moment to take relatively sober stock and plot your excuse for tomorrow's sick day.

4pm
T-Bar, Dig Your Own Rave. As the name suggests, this is the place to get down and dirty in the knowledge that what you are doing to yourself is utterly wrong. Head inside to find big names like Luciano or the Crosstown Rebels residents playing 'forward-thinking dance music' to a hedonistic crowd, causing deeply tribal, primitive-looking dancefloor action. A blessedly spacious soft seating area helps cushion the evening's early casualties, and offers an arena for the likeminded to relay competitive stories of up-all-night itineraries. Take your t-shirt off and test your disco mettle.

9:30pm
Emerge onto Bethnal Green Road and, if you still have the use of your arms, hail a cab. Sit back and harken the angel sitting on your shoulder saying 'Now, there is still time. You could be in bed by 10'. 'Or' says the fellow on the other side, 'you could tell the good man to take you to Sosho.'

10pm
Retox at Sosho. The definitive Sunday destination venue. Those who have made it this far from the night before are practically clinging together to sustain verticality, while Sosho beknights these crusaders with medallions of house, techno and electro. The hardcore crowd mixes with glossy Euro-fash poseurs attracted by the slick décor and sophistication of the cocktail menu, but by 12am the dancefloor is writhing indecently and by 3am you're likely to have borrowed someone else's pink cowboy hat, found a free place to stay if you are ever in Barcelona, and developed a wildly ambitious business plan with the bartender. Be warned though, the waitresses will keep asking you to get off the tables.

6am
Carriages. Rejoice or repent, its all over.

Public Life
82a Commercial Street
E1 6LY

T-Bar
56 Shoreditch High Street
E1 6JJ

Sosho
2 Tabernacle Street
EC2A 4LU

You'll go to The Old Queen's Head and fall in love a little bit. You'll want some more, you'll miss it when it's not around and you'll start to go every weekend.

At some point you'll think, "Hmm, this isn't very original of me, and maybe not terribly healthy either. Perhaps I should try something new?" But you won't. It's like a giant youth club for adults – you go every week, pay your subs and have fun, pure fun, in the company of like-minded hedonists. Only instead of table tennis and Space Invaders, they've got first-rate DJs (think Groove Armada, Norman Jay, Fingathing playing low-key sets in low-key surroundings for not much more than your average youth club subs (generally around £3).

People have got their fingers and toes in any number of pies, which means line-ups so varied that your whirlwind romance will stay fresher than the other side of the pillow for years to come.

Carla yells, "Let's do flavoured shots!"

On a frickin' school night, mayhem ensues, sickies are pulled. This tiny underground gig venue is home to artrocker.com and promnightuk.com. Frequented by Kiefer Sutherland – if it's good enough for Jack Bauer, it's good enough for us.

Old Queen's Head
44 Essex Road
N1 8LN
020 7354 9993
www.theoldqueenshead.com

Buffalo Bar
259 Upper Street
N1 1RU
020 7359 6191
www.buffalobar.co.uk

b **A** *re-brick walls*
two floo **R** *s of very cool stuff*
lighting, furn **I** *ture, design toys*
and **A** *great coffeeshop*

Aria
Barnsbury Hall
Barnsbury Street
N1 1PN
020 7704 6222
Mon-Wed 10am-6.30pm
Thu 10am-7pm
Fri-Sat 10am-6.30pm
Sun 12pm-5pm

It's a simple idea.

You buy one of their cards, bung some money on it and then try-before-you-buy on a range of more than 60 wines. The Chateau Haute Briton is the most expensive at £48 a taster, but most of the wines are far more affordable. A sip of Montepulciano d"Abruzzo, for instance, will set you back a mere 26p. Once you've chosen your favourite tipple, much larger bottle-sized samples are available in the shop.

The

The Sampler
266 Upper Street
N1 2UQ
020 7226 9500
Mon-Sat 11.30am-9pm
Sun 1-8pm

It may be the venue that bands hire out when they want you to know they're all grown-up and serious now (but can't afford the Albert Hall).

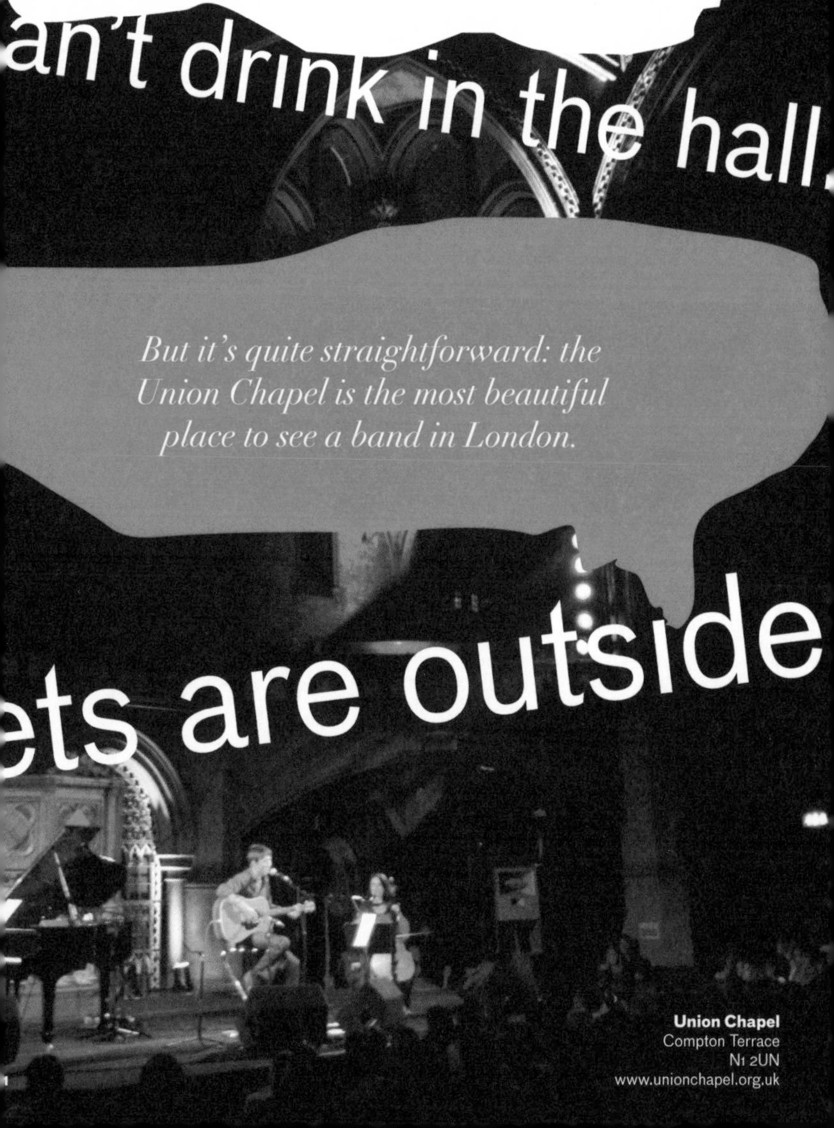

an't drink in the hall.

But it's quite straightforward: the Union Chapel is the most beautiful place to see a band in London.

ets are outside

Union Chapel
Compton Terrace
N1 2UN
www.unionchapel.org.uk

A hundred and fifty years ago, a trainee architect named Tom was given the ghoulish task of relocating the graves of Old St Pancras Church yard, which had been rudely disrupted by the arrival of the Midland Railway. The tracks sliced through the slums of Agar Town with as little regard for the dead as they did for the living who were made homeless by the iron horse. Passengers complained that the revolution of skeletons protruding from the ploughed earth was spoiling their arrival at the magnificent fairytale palace of St Pancras Station. And so Tom painstakingly reinterred the bodies, fastidiously arranging the gravestones around a young ash tree. He soon gave up his day job while the tree flourished over the decades, its roots entwining and fusing with the headstones, so that it became impossible to tell where the tree finished and the stones began. Thomas is better remembered today as one of the giants of English literature – the author of Under the Greenwood Tree among others, while the tree is named the Hardy Tree in his honour, one of the most uniquely macabre spectacles in London. Skulking in the shadow of the imposing Victorian Hospital of Tropical Diseases, this holy site is now a public garden yet retains a tranquil ancient melancholy, dripping with curious history. Dickens sent Jerry Cruncher 'fishing' here in a Tale of Two Cities – for corpses rather than fish from the Fleet River that once ran past the church but is now buried along with the dead. Shelley wooed the young Mary Wollstonecraft, author of Frankenstein, over her parents' grave. The great clown Grimaldi is buried here as is Sir John Soane, architect of the Bank of England: his family tomb became the unlikely inspiration for the design of the iconic red telephone box. More recently, the Beatles dropped by for a photo-shoot during their twilight years – that's the church yard's railings they're peering through on the centrefold of the Red

Sea salt chocolate?
Marmite Guinness Ganache?
Port and Stilton chocolate?

Down Camden Passage, past that French/Frost snooty boutique where you can never afford anything, is a place for jaded palates.

Step on in...

Paul A Young
33 Camden Passage
N1 8EA

You'll need a child for this one.

If you don't have any, borrow a niece or nephew. It's worth it, honest. Cos you'll never see this many smiling faces anywhere else.

Even in a throbbing metropolis like London,

it can be pretty tough to get a late coffee anywhere outside of Soho. Fewer still are the places where you can enjoy your preferred refreshment beneath a painting of a pair of breasts so huge that you can't stop staring at them, even if you want to. Located up winding stairs above the Candid Galleries, this hip little cafe-cum-restaurant has both a painting of huge breasts, and is open every night until 10pm. Even better, the endearingly abrupt staff are surprisingly relaxed about chucking-out time. Who needs Soho?

Little Angel Theatre
14 Dagmar Passage
Islington
N1 2DN
020 7226 1787

Candid Café
3 Torrens St, EC1V 1NQ
020 7837 4237
www.candidarts.com
Mon-Sat 12-10pm, Sun 12-5pm

Rollergirls

"There's nothing to prepare you for skating in front of a crowd of 400 people—the adrenaline is amazing and everyone feels a little shaky for their first jam, but hearing the roar when you pass through the pack, or when you get knocked down, is awesome."

So says Sky Rockit, organiser and star of le cool's favourite London sport: roller derby. Thrills, spills and girls called things like Rose Hynol and Kitty DeCapitate greviously bodily harming each other on rollerskates.

www.londonrollergirls.com

If Mark Twain was right that golf is a good walk spoiled <u>City Bunker</u> neatly does away with the problem by cutting out the walking.

You casually whack the balls at a screen that shows one of 60 famous courses, then, having exerted yourself to the max by standing in one place, you can lean back and order a cocktail or two. For those too lazy even to stand up, there's always the poker tables.

City Bunker
Cannon Workshops
Hertsmere Road
Canary Wharf
E14 4AS
020 7537 7940
www.citybunker.co.uk

Circus Training

The massive circus school in Hoxton hides in broad daylight like a lion on tiptoes. It's the only school of its kind in the UK, once you've tried a class, your previous inflexible self will never look back. Utterly beloved by its professional and amateur members alike, where the hell else do you get to take tumbling classes in one room, while down the hall hordes of Japanese kids squeak with delight while dangling from one leg on a trapeze?

Circus Space
Coronet Street
N1 6HD
020 7613 4141
www.thecircusspace.co.uk

You've beaten all your friends at those up-til-6am Dealer's Choice matches in someone's front room. You've worked your way up online from the $5/$10 rooms to the 'no limit' tables. You've even won a satellite or two.

Want to find out if you're really as good as you think you are? Come visit Gutshot.

Gutshot
44-48 Clerkenwell Rd
EC1M 5PS
020 7253 9980
www.gutshot.com

It's a long way down. The view from the top of the Castle Climbing Centre's Rockley wall is vertiginous enough to give you a real sense of achievement. And to wonder how you're going to get down again... But there's always someone to lend a hand at the friendliest of London's climbing walls (and it's set in a bloody great castle in Stoke Newington).

Castle Climbing Centre
271 Green Lane
N4 2HA
020 8211 7000

Is there a better place to eat out than the mighty SGR (Stroud Green Road)? The La Porchetta pizzeria, Pappagone's big, open, Italian-family feel, a Columbian, a Greek, a noodle bar, and the Chez Liline fish restaurant. To quote this street's MySpace page (yep, apparently streets have MySpace pages now), "F**k this Top 5 malarky, you'd need a top 50 to fit in all the ace places you can find on the SGR." Well maybe not 50 – here's four.

The Old Dairy used to be to the Friern Manor Dairy Company (look out for murals depicting dairy-farm life, including a six-fingered milkmaid), but has been pulling pints of beer rather than milk for about 40 years now. Inside it's a haven of dark wood lit by red candles and the occasional grandiose chandelier. The menu, which changes daily (apart from bastions such as sausage and mash, which don't budge), merits the trip from the comfy sofa-age of the bar into the more formal dining room. The "northern European cuisine with French/Spanish influences" works well, offering dishes such as steamed hake on a bed of spicy chickpea, coriander and chorizo with aioli.

Jai Krishna is the jewel of Stroud Green Road. Its dedicated staff (employed there for a significant chunk of the restaurant's 27-year history) serve veggie Indian food that is both cheap and bloody fantastic. The way it works is that you write your own order on the pad, and take it up to the counter. Why go for onion bhaji when you could have a potato, spinach, cauliflower, paneer or aubergine bhaji? Why get a bhaji when you could get an Indian pizza (utthappam or a delicious dosa? Jus don't fill up on deep-frie fare, as you won't have room for your pumpkin curry, described by one punter as tasting "like Israel and Palestine getting on."

Don't let the large panther put you off. Perched above Cats Café's doorway a la Catford Cat, this feline statue roars at passers below. The bizarre bric a-brac continues inside making even the staff softly cringe ("It's a bit much"). There's a John Lennon bust and a Tom ('n' Jerry) statue above the bottle-brimming ba a tuk-tuk car that takes the whole front left-har section of the premises and tables that are peppered with daringly

The Old Dairy
1-3 Crouch Hill
N4 4AP
020 7263 3337

Jai Krishna
161 Stroud Green Rd
N4 3PZ
020 7272 1680
Buy your booze beforehand
from Jack's across the road

Cats Café des Artistes
79 Stroud Green Rd
N4 3EG
020 7281 5557

Petek Restaurant
96 Stroud Green Rd
N4 3EG
020 7619 3933

"This is not a toy shop"

So the sign reads on the cobwebby door by Gospel Oak station.

And it's not.

What it is:

A Lilliputian world of doll's houses and furniture, every surface covered with 40 years' worth of tiny works of art – miniature coal scuttles, plates of food, pets and puppets.

The personal fiefdom of Kristen Baybars herself, 40 years making everything by hand and still full of the wonder of it all.

A workshop, a showroom and a museum.

One of the most oddly beautiful places in London. If this were an art exhibition – ten thousand intricately crafted household items, arranged across rooms and benches and display cases – it would be a national treasure, on display in Tate Britain or the British Museum.

Instead it's here, on Mansfield Road, behind a cobwebby door with a sign that reads "This is not a toy shop".

Kristen Baybars
7 Mansfield Road
NW3 2JD

ght yellow and orange
kins. The story goes
the owner, a Mr
d, was married to a
i woman whose name
Meaw, which sounds
"miaow". They liked
s anyway, and so the
aurant's occasional
me was born. As
as the assorted
iture plus vehicle, the
aurant's chefs come
n Thailand and the
king is very good
ed, especially the
ng rolls.

't worry if a bulb
vs, there must be
lamps hanging from
ek's ceiling. Rock up
n unusual time of day
n the restaurant is
oty (yet open) and
ll be forgiven for
ing slightly unwanted.
vever, once in,
vice-with-a-smile sets
nd dishes of pickled
es and salsa with
asket of warm,

crusty Turkish bread
are swiftly brought to
your table. Petek is best
known for its generous
portions, with many

dishes resembling Mount
Ararat on a plate. Try
their perfectly crisp
borak and dip into the
tastiest Baba Ghanoush
in town. Follow this
mini-sensation with a
mountain of kebab, salad,
humus and couscous.

As industry types start telling record shops that they have to expand and become venues, internet stores, record labels, magazine shops and meeting places in order to survive, the folks at Pure Groove shrug their shoulders and get on with it. After all, their little shop is already a venue, and an internet store and a record label and a magazine shop and a meeting place.

Pure Groove
679 Holloway Road
N19 5SE

In summer 2008, Pure Groove moved to Farringdon.

6-7 West Smithfield
EC1A 9JX
www.puregroove.co.uk

The middle land between upscale Turkish cuisine and dirty late-night kebab is the Crystal Charcoal House on Holloway Road. You can grab a takeaway or sit down for a bite. Decorated with Turkish art (kitschy images of the homeland and the odd artefact), the back eating room is consistently packed with big families, posh white folk and hipsters alike. We like the falafel platter, which comes with rice or red couscous, vegetable stew, fresh (and we mean FRESH) in-house falafel balls and salad (£5!), plus there's the chicken stew, and of course the various charcoal-roasted kebabs. Homemade hummus, a basket of flatbreads, pickled peppers and olives come with everything, so stuff yourself like an aubergine and check out a flick at the Odeon across the street afterwards.

The Crystal Charcoal House
522 Holloway Road
N7 6JP
020 7281 2846

As you'll quickly learn, this place is now the stuff of legend for victoriously battling off the Evil Developers who wanted to turn it into offices and cheap maisonettes just a few years back. Thank crunchie this David of a pub did the smack-down on Goliath because it means this local favourite, a visual homage to the then-exotic, spiky fruit that so captured the Victorian imagination, remains in all of its Victorian splendour. Etched glass, velvet booths, bric-a-brac, a garden if you fancy a fag, pub quizzes and booze. Ignore the fairly pointless gastro fare, and you'll be laughing.

The Pineapple
51 Leverton Street
NW5 2NX
020 7284 4631

This sweet lil' juke joint set away from the throng has DJs playing everything from rockabilly to current indie, all to a convivial vibe. Shane MacGowan's second home, this also is the place that reunited Pete and Carl, and saw Kate Moss pull pints behind the bar.

The Boogaloo
312 Archway Road
N6
020 8340 2928
www.theboogaloo.co.uk

Crouch End might just be the best place to eat out in London; some say it that is has more restaurants per square foot than anywhere else in Europe. It is to restaurants what Shoreditch is to nightclubs; there's something for every taste, plenty to avoid, and an international feel to proceedings. Here's how to pick the right spot: roll a dice.

1. The King's Head. Not just one of the oldest comedy venues in England, but also home to a good collection of beers, a decent kitchen, and a chatty atmosphere.

2. Le Bistro. Crouch End is spoilt for French restaurants, with Aix probably preferable for a romantic dinner and Les Associes nice for its rustic

atmosphere. Le Bistro wins for a social night out though, with a very reasonably priced set menu, outstanding food and the inevitable "couple more drinks" turning into a night of conversation.

3. Pick More Daisies. Cali cuisine and themed nights - Kobe burgers, Cobb salad, American National Holiday celebrations (you can pay in dollars) and of course everything is fresh daily, from local markets.

The King's Head
2 Crouch End Hill
N8 8AA
020 8340 1028

Le Bistro
36 Hornsey High Street
N8 7NX
020 8340 2116

Pick More Daisies
12 Crouch End Hill
N8 8AA, 020 8340 2288

Freeman's Butchers
9 Topsfield Parade
Tottenham Lane
N8 8PR
020 8340 3100

Hot Pepper Jelly
11 Broadway Parade
N8 9DE
020 8340 4318

Banner's
21 Park Road
N8 020 8348 2930

4. Hot Pepper Jelly.
This place makes their own hot pepper jams, marmalades, cakes, and boasts a menu offering almost anything you'd want with chilli, and few things you wouldn't – peanut butter, hot chocolate, mayo. Also a great spot for breakfast.

5. Freeman's Butchers.
Why not DIY with a BBQ? Freeman's wins the nod for meats because the sausages (all organic, of course) are amazing.

6. Banner's.
The Crouch End standard, with fusion cuisine, media types hovering about drinking

fancy coffee, screaming kids on weekends, punk posters on the walls.

You need a particular kind of place for afternoon drinking. A bit off the main drag, tucked away from the suits talking business, dark and warm and complicated with the feel of its own little world. Locals drift in and out, diving into the corners with the papers and dogs. You order wine – you won't last the afternoon on beer. And so it begins.

Arches
7 Fairhazel Gardens
NW6 3QE
020 7624 1867

Strictly speaking, this joint's Hungarian, but it's about the closest thing to an English tea parlour you'll find in these post-Starbucks days. It's small, wood-panelled, the cakes come on a tray, tea comes by the pot and your selection of sandwiches is generally limited to ham and cheese or cheese and tomato. All confections (from the meringues to the poppy-seed pastries) are made on the premises, loos are out the door and to your left. If you're from out of town, it is hands down one of the warmest foreign experiences you'll have on a sojourn to the Big Smoke. If you live here, then it introduces a much-needed sense of civility to the noisy city. In two words: old school.

Louis Patisserie
32 Heath Street
NW3 6TE
020 7435 9908

The Camden Arts Centre is an unexpected joy to behold, given it's found halfway down the smoggy Finchley Road (and not in Camden Town itself), one of the busiest traffic arteries into central London. An old Victorian school house that was recently completely refurbished, its curatorial programme is spot on. The quality of the work is always surprising and impressive, but each show is also presented with thoughtfulness and care – as if the work was made for the space. Its quiet, unpretentious and spacious layout offers a really natural-feeling setting for this small but perfectly formed gallery experience. Together with a lovely cafe (with wifi), rambling garden (full of daffodils in the spring), discriminating but excellent bookshop, artist residencies and a programme of evening classes and short courses in drawing and ceramics, it's an understated treat. I also discovered the work of Bas Jan Ader there, and haven't looked back.

Camden Arts Centre
Arkwright Road
NW3 6DG
020 7472 5500
Tues-Sun 10am-6pm
Wed 10am-9pm
Late opening every
Wednesday until 9pm
includes free talks, film
screenings and live art
performances. www.
camdenartscentre.org

It's pub of two halves. In the winter it's yer classic London hideyhole. Writerly types drink afternoon pints till the rain stops. Various Monty Pythons try to avoid having their past quoted back at them. Groups commandeer the booths and order wine by the bottle. Everyone's getting quietly smashed. But come summer the action's all outside. There's gotta be more schools within a ten-minute walk of The Flask then virtually any pub in the city and it shows. The green outside is dotted with all of the capital's youth tribes - scoping each other out and sending the tallest one in for "Sixteen pints and a bag of crisps" in his deepest voice.

The Flask
77 Highgate West Hill
N6 6BU

Stokey naysayers beware. Church Street's Saturday morning organic farmers market and barrage of three-wheeled, 300 quid-a-pop baby buggies certainly fuels its reputation as Hackney and Dalston's more salubrious older sister. But the truth is, it's fun being fly. And if you know what you're doing, it can cost you next to nowt. Sirs, Madams, this is how one does Stoke Newington on the cheap.

Award winning, cutting edge, the Arcola Arts Theatre is a former factory, and was founded eight years ago by Artistic Director Mehmet Ergen and Executive Producer Leyla Nazli. One of the most trusted fringe venues in the city,

not only is Arcola the world's first carbon-neutral theatre complete with eco-friendly bar, but most Tuesdays it runs a "Pay What You Can" policy for evening plays.

Pub frequenters can go one of two ways,

the cheaper Rochester Castle (with obvious ambience) or if, you fancy pushing up the pennies for a pint, The Londesborough – a lovely, smoochy, relaxed local. On the hedonistic flip, and for only a fiver before midnight, Disco Bloodbath is held once a month down the Amhurst Road, at the infamous Alig-inspired, dirty dive all-nighter Caribbean social club Passion.

In the single half-mile stretch where Stoke Newington Road runs into Stoke Newington

High Street, 16 Turkish estaurants advertise he wonders of ahmacun. Maybe we could wax eloquent about this sincere Anatolian flatbread wrap, grilled-to-a-crisp, fragrantly spiked with chilli, garlic, parsley and mince lamb? Or simply tell you it's £1.50 for the pleasure at Anatolia, a favourite late-night ahmacun spot, minutes from the always-reliable, 24-hour Bagel House.

Next day, the perfect trinity to cure bleary-eyed, morning-after blues is fresh coffee, fresh air and dusty secondhand records.

Stroll down Stoke Newington Church Street straight to the Spence Bakery, whose unmistakable orange façade beams a beacon for sense-awakening coffee, perfumed cakes (the blueberry cheesecake is a dream) and freshly baked loaves. And 30 metres away, hidden in the back room of Ocean Books, is a secret cave of secondhand vinyl, graciously worn records from post-punk to hip hop splayed over every available surface and starting at a just pound a pop. The end of the road welcomes the breezy oasis of Clissold Park; its vast glorious greens, grazed in part by deer and mountain goats who seem nonchalant to the 25,000 festival goers that descend every June for the free summer music and arts festival, Stokefest. Stoke Newington, it's priceless.

Arcola Theatre
27 Arcola Street
E8 2DJ
020 7503 1646
www.arcolatheatre.com

The Londesborough
36 Barbauld a
N16 0SS
020 7254 5865

Passion
251 Amhurst Road
N16 7UN
www.myspace.com/
discobloodbathdisco

Anatolia
170 Stoke Newington Road
N16 7UY
020 7254 4291

The Bagel House
2 Stoke Newington High Street
N16 7PL
020 7249 3908

The Spence Bakery
161 Stoke Newington Church
Street
N16 0UL
020 7249 4927

Ocean Books
127 Stoke Newington Church
Street
N16 0UH
020 7502 6319

Clissold Park
Stoke Newington Church Street
N16 5HJ
www.stokefest.co.uk

It's something like being enveloped in a huge warm Vicks inhaler.

Spa London's eucalyptus steam room is both weirdly invigorating and worryingly medicinal. From out of a green sci-fi mist, figures emerge – but they're not the usual old buffers you get in these grand saunas, as these 1920s baths are actually council run. That's what you've got to love about the place – there's currently a whole new sweaty generation trying out the Turkish baths (you can tell who the newbies are by the screams from the cold plunge pool). There's lots of your posh 21st-century treatments – hot-stones massage and Micronised Marine Algae Body Wrap – but what you're here for is the baths, classic white-tiled steam rooms, heated benches and blasts of wet heat that, if you close your eyes, will transport you from rainy Bethnal Green to the heart of the rainforest.

Hackney

Spa London
York Hall Leisure Centre
Old Ford Road
E2 9PJ
020 8709 5845
www.spa-london.org

Vyner Street

Vyner Street has more galleries on it than any other in London. A particularly strange fact given that, when you arrive, what you'll see first is a nondescript East End sidestreet filled with garages doing black-cab repairs, windows showing rooms of oriental ladies making fabrics, a locals-only pub, and some desultory youths hanging around the social housing at the end. But hold on, what's that on the corner of Mowlem Street, behind a narrow glass front?

There are fifteen or so Vyner Street galleries. Most of the time, you'll need to ring a bell to access them, but if you arrive on the first Thursday of the month, doors are opened, **shows are previewed**, and the street fills with so many people that it feels like a party.

Just wander into a gallery, get a beer from a plastic bin, and look around. Hoxton trendies, art students, gallery owners and artists mix with interested punters until around 9pm, when the galleries start closing and everyone heads for that locals-only pub on the corner. It's called **The Victory**, and it's a classic boozer with Victorian woodwork and a pool table. Not that there's room for a game – once the art lovers arrive, the place gets packed, and the crowd spills into the cul-de-sac outside.

Gallery Guide

Arriving from Cambridge Heath Road, the first gallery is <u>Alma Enterprises</u>. It usually contains **group shows**, mixing anything from installations to video pieces.

To see more established artists, try the excellent <u>Modern Art</u> at number 10, or the small <u>Kate McGarry Gallery</u> opposite, or **VINEspace** in that cul-de-sac by the pub.

While you are down there, <u>Nettie Horn</u> has consistently good shows, and if <u>Lime Wharf</u> is open, you'll discover one of the more unusual spaces on Vyner Street, a long gallery stretching along the canal that runs behind the street. The tiny <u>Lorem Ipsum Gallery</u> across the road shows particularly oblique stuff, and opposite the pub, <u>The Empire</u> at number 30 lays on often-brilliant student showcases in a converted loft accessed by steep stairs.

32a Vyner Street hosts <u>Artists Anonymous</u> – they were once evicted from this location, and turned the experience into a tense piece of video art. It ended happily, **though, and they managed to return to their space,** where they continue to offer work that swings from the outrageously awful to the mind-spinningly fantastic.

45 Vyner Street is an address with no less than three galleries inside, small, cool white spaces whose minimalism feels tailored to attract international collectors' money. **The biggest gallery,** <u>The Wilkinson</u>, is opposite; its opening in 2007 marked a watershed for Vyner Street - the arrival of an architect-designed, top-level destination gallery on a par with Hoxton's White Cube or Kings Cross's Gagosian, with modern facilities and capable of mounting headline shows. Two huge floors of gallery space and a studies room are contained in a warehouse refurb, all behind a huge black wall broken with a cantilevered gallery window high above the street (which is a great place to watch the crowds from on a busy evening).

Broadway Market
Between London Fields and Regent's Canal
Saturday 9am-5pm for the farmers' market

The jewel in the crown that is E8, Broadway Market is situated in the heart both of London Fields and of the local residents. With the best coffee this side of Mare Street, organic goodies aplenty, and cheeky vintage numbers for when you need to impress down the Dragon Bar, it's one of the best pockets of London for seeing a proper slice of East End life. Fabulous stalls sell funky flowers, veg, smoothies, crêpes, African stew, and pie and mash (of course). The film shop is quirky and not for the uneducated (it's all ordered by director, dahling), the knitwear massive try to outdo each other in wearing big sweaters while the local artists over-conceptualise over delirium tremens. Other highlights? Pumping reggae from the Jamaican fish shop, the French crêpe guy, carrot cake and people-watching. And the Dove pub and the Cat and Mutton are brilliant boozers. Get over there for a bit of Hackney Spirit; it's come a long way in the last decade.

This dowdy Irish pub on the delightfully dingy Mare Street in Hackney is worth a visit, primarily if you're drunk, lost, or in the mood for singing 'These Boots Are Made For Walking' very, very loudly. On the weekend this is a raucous karaoke pub, and your audience will consist of rough-and-ready locals plus half the lacquered fringes and neon fabrics of east London's trendy night scene. In short, this is the place to turn to when everything in Shoreditch is closed and there's little else to do but sing.

The Dolphin
165 Mare Street
E8 3RH
020 8985 3727

Late mornings in the courtyard.
Hangovers, the Sunday papers and familiar faces.
Warhol on the big screen, Alexander McQueen
having a drink. Early evening lobster 'n' chips in
the restaurant, late evening mojitos at the bar.

Late night at the cabaret.
Johnny Woo is making the drag queens scream
while trannies drape themselves over the piano.
Bistrotheque time.

Bistrotheque
23-27 Wadeson Street
E2 9DR
020 8983 7900
www.bistrotheque.com
Brunch Sat & Sun 11am-4pm
Dinner Sun-Thu 6:30pm-10.30pm, Fri & Sat 6.30pm-11pm

Vietnamese Row
When Uncle Ho
began his struggle for
independence in the
40s, he hardly knew

his actions would result
in the scattering of
industrious Vietnamese
the world over. Luckily
for Londoners, a number
have settled down and
opened up shop in
Shoreditch and Hackney.
With a sprinkling on
Kingsland Road, and
another handful on

Mare Street, there is an
extensive selection for
you pho lovers.

Song Quê – named for a

popular Vietnamese song
about a homeland river.
134 Kingsland Road,
E2. Order the bun bo
huê (spicy beef noodle
soup), Vietnamese
pancakes, summer rolls,
spicy squid, and betel-
leaf beef. The soft-shell
crabs are the best in the
area.

Tre Viet, Hackney
E8 has a number of
incarnations – but go to
the original at 251 Mare
St. Their BBQ pork bún

(Steamed vermicelli with
fish sauce, nuts, some
veg and a springroll) is
legendary.

The Vietnamese Canteen
on Englefield Road. They
are rude as you like, it
takes ages to get served,
but you can get a whole
steamed sea bass for £7.

BGWMC
44-46 Pollard Road
E2 6NB
020 7739 7170

BGWMC

The Bethnal Green Working Men's Club is one of the few places where you can actually visualise the sweaty dancehalls your parents might have been groped in as teenagers. Monthly night Grind-A-Go-Go is a seedy wrong mess of sixties throwbacks
and curious newcomers, mingling languidly among knackered furniture. A couple of
lacklustre go-go dancers shimmy on rotating plates while oily-moustached chaps hud-
dle at the bar wearing varying shades of brown. Sixties pop of the non-cheesy variety
dominates the speakers, and there's a bit of striptease to close each evening. A most
satisfying night of oddball glamour, if you don't mind a frolic amid the stink of vintage
armpit. And the cross-dressing glass collector is a lovely chap.

For Alices in Wonderland and Rainbow Brites, sparkle-lidded teens and vintage prom queens, the ambrosial <u>Tatty Devine</u> holds a special trouvaille for you all. With mini 12-inches to dangle from the wrist, Cinderella carriages in reflective silhouette and mirror-linked headbands for crowns, it's a fantasia for the glitter magpies. Even the old-enough-to-know-betters skulking by the more sensible pieces find infantine succour among the cartoon spectres and kiddy-cat bangles.

Tatty Devine
236 Brick Lane
E2 7EB
020 7739 9191
Tues–Sun, 11am-6pm

57b Brewer Street
W1F 9UR
020 7434 2257
Mon–Sat, 11am-7pm, Sun 12pm-5pm
www.tattydevine.com

Not the place for a quiet cuppa. Within five minutes, owner Nev has read the papers over the shoulders of various customers, discussed the news, offered everyone in the place a bet on the football and given someone a slice of his mum's jam tart cos "it doesn't seem right to have a cup of tea on its own." It's a straight-up, 24-carat slice of London life – the kind of formica'ed family-run caff that you used to find on every corner. But it's not nostalgia that makes E Pellici so popular. It's the classic combo of English caff food and Italian dishes made in the back room by Nev's mum, a crowd who all know each other and staff who know 'em even better.

E Pellicci
332 Bethnal Green Road
E2
020 7739 4873

Some pubs are just pubs.
Nothing wrong with that. We ♥ pubs.
Some pubs are pubs and organic beer houses and performance spaces and art galleries and salons and ping-pong venues and DJ bars and restaurants and free wifi hotspots.

Definitely nothing wrong with that.
We ♥ the Fleapit too.

The Fleapit
49 Columbia Road
E2 7RG
0871 971 3441
Tues-Sat 11am-11pm, Sun 9am-2pm

From: ▮▮▮▮▮▮▮▮▮▮▮▮▮
Date: ▮▮▮▮▮▮▮▮▮▮▮▮
Subject: Restaurants
To: ▮▮▮▮▮▮▮▮▮@gmail.com
Cc: ▮▮▮▮▮▮▮▮@▮▮▮▮▮▮

Hi ▮▮▮▮

I found some time to stick some stuff down in writing as have had a call cancelled.

I'm just going to list the places and put a couple of words in explanation with each, my favourites are starred***.

Vietnamese -

Song Que, Kingsland Road - Large, Bright, Cheap, Excellent Quality & Value. I think the best place on Kingsland Road for Vietnamese

***Vietnamese Canteen, Englefield Road N1 - Really feels like a proper Hanoi dive, its also a Vietnamese community centre, they are rude as you like, it takes ages to get served, but there is a whole steamed sea bass for £7 which I have found is impossible to do at this price at home. Other amazing dishes include the Vietnamese pancake and there is a mind blowing aubergine thing too. This place has become a bit trendy recently - you end up sitting next to ~~Peaches Geldof~~ or some other west London ~~prick~~ which makes me want to vomit - and so it's always rammed and you need to book.

Tre Viet, *Mare St*, Hackney E8 - Very near ▮▮▮ house, I ate here twice a week for years, the food is a good quality, perhaps not quite *good as the* two above but it gets a mention because of the bbq pork with rice vermicelli which is killer. BYO

Turkish

The impression I get from people in Dalston is that you are generally a fan of one of two Turkish places but both are exceptional.

***Number 19 (Numera 19 Bos Cirric) Stoke Newington Road - Ocakbasi. There are three branches of this place, the Dalston one is the original and best. Its very basic in terms of décor, all about the meat - the lamb ribs are wonderful, ~~as is~~ pretty much everything. The yoghurt kebabs are worth a try - a kebab cooked in a spicy tomato and yoghurt sauce in the oven. They bring out lots of free salads too go alongside your meat, including one made from char grilled onion in pomegranate molasses. Bread is grilled under the meat to soak up the juices. BYO

Mangal, Dalston - There are three all around the corner from each other, the smallest and original one is in Arcola St, Gilbert & George eat here a lot, its very good, but a bit less comfortable than Number 19. I have only eaten here once.

Also worth a mention is another Turkish restaurant in Dalston called Somine, which is just stews and rice - but all excellent, you can eat here for a fiver per person.

'Food of the Indian sub-continent' -

I haven't eaten many meals in Brick Lane, the ones I have were forgettable, but south of Whitechapel high st there are two brilliant places -

Lahore Kebab House, Umberston St, E2 - Enormous, canteen style Pakistani curry joint. Very short and basic menu, heavy on meat (mutton curry on the bone is particularly good), the lamb chops are a great starter to share. BYO.

Tayab, Fieldgate St E2, Like Lahore only a bit smarter and full of Shoreditch ▮▮▮▮, slightly more expensive (food still great though) and *the staff are very rude*. Despite the short-comings I ~~would~~ recommend it.

Rasa, Stoke Newington Church St, N16. Bright *Pink* Vegetarian Keralan restaurant. Fresh light flavours, excellent value (the Kerala feast is £18 per person) my favourite dishes *are* the beetroot curry, the creamy aubergine curry and there is a black eye bean thing too but everything is faultless and very imaginative. The guy is quite famous now, ▮▮▮▮▮ ▮▮▮▮ thinks his cookbook is 'Wicked' - Twat.

Caribbean

Peppers & Spice, Kingsland Road, E8 - Outstanding Caribbean takeaway serving Jerk, Curry Goat (which you can cut with a sponge), Stew Mutton, home made patties. Has a queue out the door all day, every day. Puts anywhere else in the shade.

Fancy Restaurants -

Bistrotheque - hyper trendy, 'edgy' Hackney restaurant in a warehouse serving bistro classics to the media whores of south Hackney. There is a bar downstairs and a cabaret room (of course there is..).

LMNT - Bizarre and wonderful French restaurant on a really run down road (Queensbridge Road). Until 6pm starters are all 2.95 and mains are £6.95, then the prices increase slightly but still incredible value. The cooking is French inspired. The room is nuts, you can seated in an enormous teacup, or up a ladder in the corner. Its all mock-Egyptian weirdness, and there is hard core pornography in the loos. I went for a long lunch there recently - we had bubbles then three courses with lots of wine, including a sticky, and coffee and water, and I had an Armagnac and it came to less than £30 each.

Thai

Charlie Wrights, Pitfield St

Ask ▮▮▮▮▮ he thinks a place in Finsbury Park is better, but he's wrong. This is a pub with Thai food, so its real cheap, but very very fresh and good quality. Also this place is only a couple of minutes round the corner from the new Primus office so you'll have to sort it out and make people go there.

That should keep you going for a bit

▮▮▮▮ I copied you so you can get fat on my recommendations)

This former 1920s electricity showroom is now a two-fold house of fun on the way into Hoxton Square. Upstairs, high ceilings soar above a sort of hunting lodge/country club scene offset by illuminated red alcoves. Various outmoded treats cover the walls, including the classic three-duck formation so dear to our nation's hearts. Along one side, a bank of large windows swing open in the summer months, letting the Hoxtonites spill out a little closer to their beloved square while getting steadily more hammered.

Electricity Showrooms
39a Hoxton Square
N1
020 7739 3939

You'd never guess that this relatively sedate bar would hide a Saturday Night Fever-style disco in the basement (although the Vegas-lit peacock at the top of the stairs might give you a hint). It's free to get in, and fills up with young 'uns pretty quickly, so early migration to the basement is recommended. Music varies drastically in genre and quality, and the crowd can get a tad bawdy, but once you're hopscotching merrily across its chequerboard dancefloor, none of it seems to matter. Beware of see-through fabrics on one's lower regions; the flashing floor tiles lights up undergarments a treat.

Standing outside the <u>Clown Museum</u>, you're pretty sure you've got the wrong place. It looks like a particularly dull church hall, with serious grills on the window and a blink-and-you'd-miss-it buzzer. Inside, everything's different. The clowns running this place (not meant in the pejorative sense, obviously) are pottering around, making tea and entertaining the kids – even though they're not in make-up or costume, you can just tell who's a clown just from their faces. There's a room crammed with exhibits – piles of giant shoes, clown videos – but the real joy is the egg collection. Like snowflakes, or Victoria Beckham's outfits, no two clowns' faces can be the same. Each pattern is recorded and then painstakingly copied onto the face of a blank egg at a kind of clownish patent office. One wall is covered with a huge egg-rack, recording the faces of all clowns, past and present. All of which demonstrates that, if you want to become a clown, you have some pretty big shoes to fill.

Holy Trinity
The Clown's Church
Beechwood Road,
E8 3DY

The Hackney jackals with rolls of twenties in their drainpipes, the Stoke Newington mums in bakers' caps, a whiff of old east London from the baying stallholders and twenty shed-loads of plantlife turn <u>Columbia Road</u> into a swanky little market every Sunday. Around three in the afternoon is the time to scuttle down for a mammoth sheaf of long-stemmed blooms at a reduced price, then grab something tasty and unavoidably organic at one of the cafés. Leave it too late though, and the whole lot dwindles to some shoe-bruised gerberas and a few earthy fronds.

Columbia Road Flower Market
Columbia Road
E2
Every Sunday 8am-2pm
www.columbia-flower-market.freewebspace.com

NO FOOD OTHER THAN <u>PIE & MASH</u>

IS TO BE CONSUMED
IN THIS SHOP
THANK-YOU

G Kelly's
414 Bethnal Green Road
E2 oDJ

Senate House Malet St WC1 (Tube: Russell Square) 64m/19 storeys high. Senate House is part of the University of London whose Principal was killed by a trolley falling down a liftshaft during construction in 1936. It was the tallest skyscraper in London for 22 years and it houses a whole host of academic libraries. Rumours that Hitler planned to make it the Nazi Party HQ when he invaded are probably an urban myth, but George Orwell did base his Ministry of Truth in 1984 on this imposing stone pile.

Lloyds of London Leadenhall Street EC1 (Tube: Bank) 84m /14 storeys high. Lloyds started underwriting insurance in 1688 and 298 years later they moved into the most expensive London building yet. Richard Rogers' high-tech design is insideout architecture – all the service stuff like lifts and pipes are on show. See those stacked silver boxes with portholes? They are actually loo pods, supplied by a nuclear industry contractor. On the eleventh floor, a grand Regency room is exactly re-assembled from a great country house in Wiltshire. At night, cool colour lighting makes the building look like an alien spaceship. It's already dwarfed by the Gherkin, and soon an even taller skyscraper known as The Cheese Grater will loom over it too.

Trellick Tower Golborne Rd W10 (Tube: Westbourne Park) 98m/32 storeys high. This is the best work of Ernö Goldfinger, who Ian Fleming hated so much he named the James Bond villain after him. As soon as it opened in 1972, it was flooded by a fire hydrant, and things went downhill from there. Lifts failed, sewage backed up, fires burnt, yobs and drug dealers created a reign of terror – this was the mother of high-rise hells, with suicides and gang-rape. Now it's all cleaned up and one of the hottest property locations in London. Blur name-check it in the song Best Days.

Centre Point St Giles' Circus WC1 (Tube: Tottenham Court Road) 121m /35 storeys high. Post-war office blocks were boxy and dull, but this one actually has something of the Swinging Sixties about it – it's been called London's first Pop Art building. Designed by the late, great Richard Seifert, it was notorious for staying empty for 15 years. There was a rumour that it was a secret government HQ in case of biological war, and it was occupied by angry squatters in 1974. Its dazzling honeycomb exterior make it unique and the neon letters on the top saying CENTRE POINT are brilliant for getting orientated if you're lost or pissed.

Guy's Tower St Thomas Street SE1 (Tube: London Bridge) 144m/ 32 storeys high. This big brutalist tower is part of Guy's Hospital, and the tallest medical building in the world. That bit that sticks out at the top is actually a lecture theatre – if you sat at the back, you'd be over thin air. Inside, the dental suction system was designed to suck up to 1.2 tonnes of spit per second.

Broadgate Tower Primrose Street EC2 (Tube: Liverpool St) 164m/36 storeys high. This brand new energy-efficient shiny tower is the only London skyscraper by Adrian Smith, the guy who designed the Burj Dubai, the world's tallest building (which is about four times higher). The cross-bracing is just like the John Hancock in Chicago. It's just a stone's throw from Shoreditch, so let's hope the City skyscrapers don't continue spreading north.

Telecom Tower Howland Street W1 (Tube: Goodge Street)177m to roof/26 storeys. This mad 1960s tower is pure B-movie science fiction designed by boffins and bristling with telecoms and TV relay equipment, microwave antennae (those are the purple horns below the 'rotunda' head) and a weather mast. A revolving restaurant was at the top, where Paul McCartney once threw a party – Jimi Hendrix and Donovan dropped by. The restaurant closed in 1980 for security reasons, nine years after a Provisional IRA bomb exploded there. The Tower's location was an Official Secret until 1993.

Tower 42 Old Broad Street EC2 (Tube: Bank or Liverpool Street) 183m/47 storeys high. This was London's tallest skyscraper in 1980 and the world's tallest cantilevered building – all the floors stick out into space. It was amazing engineering, lined up with lasers and it had pressurised fire stairs – New York didn't pick up on that till after 9/11. It survived a 1993 IRA bomb that did £1 billion of damage. When you pass a NatWest bank, look at the logo – this tower has the same cross section. It used to be NatWest's HQ, but architect Richard Seifert (he of Centre Point fame) always said that was a coincidence. Yeah, sure. Book the lunch in Vertigo on the 42nd floor – it's not too pricey, considering it's the best view in London.

One Canada Square E14 (Tube: Canary Wharf) 235m/50 storeys high. This is London's tallest skyscraper, but what a cheek – American architect Cesar Pelli just recycled a tower he'd already designed in New York. Here, Cybermen and Daleks finally met, but Dr Who was in the tower to deal with them. By 2010, The Shard and The Helter Skelter will be taller.

The City

A GOOD THING IS SOON SNATCHED UP
HASTE IS SLOW
FINERY IS FOOLERY
SILENCE IS GOLDEN
WISDOM IS RARE
SEIZE OCCASION

For a pub so close to the city, the slogans in the Black Friar's Art Deco dining room seem dangerously laid back. The room is elegant, the pies are excellent, the ale is real, and the relaxed mood is infectious. This is the place for turning "a quick one at lunchtime" into a proper afternoon session.

The Black Friar
174 Queen Victoria Street
Blackfriars
EC4V 4EG

City of London Dragon Safari

Stalking dragons in the City of London – the original Square Mile – is a serious affair requiring patience, a sharp eye and keen wits. London dragons inhabit a complex world of ancient ledges, curving architectural spans and elusive corners. Just over your shoulder could lurk a fierce eye, a fleshy snout, darting tongue, claws bared beneath rising wings. Keep your camera close. You never know when you'll need it.

Boundary Dragons are the easiest catch for the amateur hunter. These fierce silver beasts — standing on plinths with upswept wings and arrowhead tongues, clutching shields bearing the red cross of St George and short sword of St Paul — guard many of the main entrances to the City of London. They stand at the south end of London Bridge and Blackfriars Bridge. They flank either side of Holborn opposite the medieval, timber-framed Staple Inn. Boundary dragons also live on the Victoria Embankment alongside the River Thames.

Remember when Lucy first stepped through the wardrobe? When Alice fell down the rabbit hole? When the Doctor picked up his latest hitchhiker?

Turn down Chancery Lane, away from the border of Westminster and the City. Dodge the sharp-elbowed suits jostling on the pavement, the clatter of traffic and the interminable rattle of roadworks. Take a step through an unassuming doorway on your right, and watch reality bend.

Under the shadow of an ancient sweet-chestnut tree, the hubbub of the 21st century fades as if someone has turned down the volume. An unsettling hush descends. Only the neatly parked BMWs and Alfa Romeos suggest you haven't tumbled hundreds of years back in time. This is Lincoln's Inn, the prettiest of London's four surviving Inns of Court.

While it might look like a film set – and it's regularly used for just that purpose – Lincoln's Inn is very much a living, breathing institution where barristers train, study, practice and, in some cases, still reside. This place is old. Really old. The appositely named Old Hall, where Dickens set the incomprehensible case of Jarndyce v Jarndyce in Bleak House, dates back as far as 1491. New Square, on the other hand, is a youthful 300-odd years old. Kids today, eh?

Inigo Jones' chapel – the only building in Lincoln's Inn that's open to the public – crouches over a raised, ground-level crypt where the feeling of cloistered calm is almost giddying. Desperate mothers were known to leave their newborn babies here, hoping – probably correctly – that they would receive a better life adopted by the Inn. The abandoned infants were often given the surname Lincoln.

Pick of a beautiful bunch of buildings is the stunning Great Hall, a neo-Tudor fortress in red and gold brick that rivals the Tower for sheer spectacle. Opened by Queen Victoria in 1845, it's now possibly the world's poshest canteen as well as a concert venue for the Bar Musical Society.

But it's the tangible tranquillity that most impresses. Friendly but firm notices warn that: "The Porters & Police have Orders to remove all Persons making a noise within this Inn", and the rambling complex - some 11 acres in total – has the palpable sense of somewhere you really ought to be on your best behaviour. Indeed, public access – only available on weekdays between 10am and 4pm – is a privilege rather than a right. Embrace it gratefully, and escape into the calm.

Lincoln's Inn
Chancery Lane
WC2A

The other Inns are essential visits too, and feature Harry Potter's dining hall and Temple Church (permanently swamped by Dan Brown fans asking if anyone's seen the Holy Grail).

Temple Bar Dragon is the tall, gothic, freestanding beast that looms over the Temple Bar Memorial on Fleet Street before the Royal Courts of Justice. It is also a boundary marker, and it is here that traditionally the ruling monarch must be welcomed by the City's Lord Mayor before entering. (The original 17th-century Temple Bar gateway is now installed between St Paul's Cathedral and Paternoster Square. Look for a lovely, well-fed dragon squatting there.) Dramatic photographs of Temple Bar Dragon can be produced against the spiky courthouse towers, or simply against a deep blue sky. On a bright day capture it in silhouette. If overcast, go for its pointy detail.

First things first. Go to the website (www.courtnews2.co.uk/courtlists/current/indexdailies.htm), scroll down to Central Criminal Court (the proper name for the Old Bailey) and see who's up before the judge. Then do a bit of googling to find out what the cases are about.

What you're looking for is not just a juicy case. Get your timing wrong and you could be there for the legal administration, so avoid anything that says 'For Plea and Directions', 'Application to Extend Custody Time Limit' or even 'Preliminary Hearing'.

What you're looking for is 'Trial: Part Heard'. That means you're going to be dropping into the heart of the matter where all the good stuff is – questioning, witnesses, accusations and spats. Check all the courts – though Court Number One is usually used for the main trial of the day, it's a bit technologically behind some of the newer ones, so interesting fraud cases often get moved somewhere smaller.

It's easy enough to spot – just look for huddled groups of hard-smokin' eastern Europeans who constantly signpost its entrance.

Downstairs, the décor is reminiscent of a Transylvanian village hall on a special occasion. Tables are laid out for big family parties, with bottles of fizzy pop, and balloons tied to the backs of chairs.

This is no theme joint or novelty act; it is full of Romanians. They stand out a mile – the guys in their shiny suits and white loafers, the gals hanging off their arms in sequined, tassel-fringed dresses and matching floral trouser-top ensembles. The waiters hardly speak English and the menu tries to tantalise you thus:

Papanasi Prajiti - Fried cheese to you.

Mititei - Typical Romanian. This is rocket fuel. In Romania we don't do coke, we don't need it because we have MITITEI!!

Weiner Schnitzel - Famous dish – has nothing to do with Romania.

But you must ignore such irrelevances, because you don't

Be there before 10am – that's when it opens, but to trump the tourists, 9.30am is a safer bet. Don't bring your camera – it won't be confiscated, you'll simply be told to leave.

Happy hunting. You might not catch a epoch-shaking trial – though Oscar Wilde, the Krays, Dr Crippen and the Yorkshire Ripper were all tried here – but you will be watching history in action. Cases have been heard on this site since the 16th century, and it's filled with strange old traditions. Watch out for the small posy of flowers carried by each judge on certain days, a tradition dating back to when Newgate Prison was situated next door, and the flowers helped cover the stench.

Old Bailey
EC4M 7EH
020 7248 3277
Mon-Fri 10am to 1pm and 2pm to 5pm
Closed Bank Holiday Mondays and the days immediately after. Reduced court sitting in August

come here for the food or the wine or the service. You come here for the three-man wedding band playing gypsy folk and cheesy pop songs. You come here to bask in the warm glow radiating from fellow diners, who sing along with the band and get up between courses to dance. And you come so that you can lose yourself in their world and forget the time and miss the last Tube home.

The Romanian Restaurant
32 Old Bailey
EC4M 7HS

For the wildest time here, keep an eye out for their live Balkan music events, listed at www.kazum.co.uk

A couple of dozen steps east on Fleet Street, notice a pair of dragons to the right of the entrance of St Dunstan's in the West church, carved into a stone panel.

When the Evening Standard Guide to London Pubs was published in the 70s they included one fictitious entry. The first person to spot it was to win a prize. Most of the replies they recieved said the answer was Ye Old Mitre.

It's easy to see why. Down an unmarked tiny alley between two City streets, you'd never come across the place unless you were seriously searching for it. And when you do find it, it seems impossible that a place with such a history could be so little known. It's been here since 1546, soon after which Queen Elizabeth (not the current one) apparently danced around the cherry tree that has pride of place inside the little wooden bar.

It's technically in Cambridgeshire (something to do with the land ownership – ask the barman – he knows all this stuff) and word has it that thieves who've robbed one of the nearby Hatton Garden jewellers hole up in there while the Met have to call out their Cambridgeshire brethren. It's not open Saturday or Sunday, except on the Olympia Beer Festival weekend.

Ye Old Mitre
1 Ely Court
(between Ely Place and Hatton Gardens)
EC1N 6SJ

The Holborn Viaduct is a veritable dragon's lair. When walking across the bridge, large pairs of tongue-waggling silver dragon heads appear above the parapets. (Clamber over the security blocks to get a closer look.) These dragons rise from giant coats-of-arms of the City, mounted centrally on each side of the viaduct. Between the dragons are some imposing jousting helmets mounted with dragon wings. At the foot of each lamppost along the viaduct sits a red dragon picked out with gold, and large winged lions guard either end.

5.02am Am at the secret butcher's pub in the bowels of Smithfield Market again. There's no better way to start the day than a couple of pints of Guinness and a plate of chips in the company of burly skinheads in bloodstained overalls. In the toilet I notice a curious advert featuring two kiwi fruits – one hairy, one freshly shaved. It takes me a while to work out that it's for a razor especially designed for shaving your gonads. Takes all sorts.

1

The Fox and Anc
15, Charterhouse St
ECiM 6AA
020 7253 5075

Smithfield Market is the largest 'dead meat' market in the country, and, like the viaduct is another Victorian celebration in stone and polychrome ironwork. The striking purples, greens and blues of the market's cast-iron skeleton are the same colours that visitors would have seen when it first opened in 1868. The market is two city blocks long, and walking around the 10-acre site reveals a wide range of dragons. Admire those crouched and ready to spring from the spandrels above either end of Grand Avenue that bisects the buildings. Contemplate the massive dragons of Portland stone squatting below the market's octagonal corner towers. A pair of prancing dragons display themselves in the playfully sculpted City coat-of-arms over the eastern entrance. Vegetarian dragon spotters may prefer to give Smithfield a pass before 10am, to avoid the carcasses being stacked into refrigerated vans.

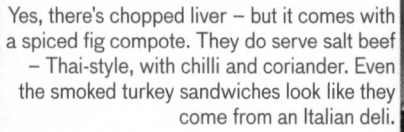

You'd expect to find a kosher restaurant jutting out of the side of one of the city's oldest (and prettiest) synagogues. You wouldn't expect it to be anything like <u>Bevis Marks</u>.

Yes, there's chopped liver – but it comes with a spiced fig compote. They do serve salt beef – Thai-style, with chilli and coriander. Even the smoked turkey sandwiches look like they come from an Italian deli.

There's an amazing Israeli wine list too, but you might prefer to pop round the corner to <u>Lowlander</u> – more than forty different beers to choose from for a post-dinner nightcap.

Bevis Marks
4 Heneage Lane
EC3A 5DQ
020 7283 2220

Lowlander
20 Creechurch Lane
EC3A 5AY
020 7623 8813

Leadenhall Market is another enchanting tribute to the Victorian combination of engineering and aesthetic whimsy. Unexpectedly tucked away off Gracechurch Street, the atmosphere within this tall, narrow space is dim and dusty, marked by an occasional stray beam of sunlight. Where the two market passages cross, iron columns rise supporting a square dome with dragons in its eaves. If you look over the entrances of the passages, you will see that dragons are cheeky enough to live there as well. These dragons cling to the high shadows, so some careful use of flash, tripod and medium-long telephoto lens might be enough tame them.

Upstairs is one of the City's most charming churches – all incense, artworks and the famous bells that cockneys are born within the sound of.

Downstairs is a crypt full of cake and coffee.

The Place Below
St Mary le Bow Church
Cheapside
EC2V 6AU
020 7329 0789

Monument, Christopher Wren's imposing Doric column commemorating the Great Fire, offers a glimpse of the oldest dragons in the City — four old beasts, weathered and startled from sleep, clinging to its pedestal. In the giant frieze, look for the City Dragon supporting a fire-ruined London on his back.

Other notable dragons: wide-eyed, spitting mad dragons at four of the entrances to Bank station; the enormous golden dragon atop St Mary le Bow Church on Cheapside; a very modern St George tilting at a three-tongued, water-spewing dragon on Dorset Rise, below Fleet Street.

Quite simply, **the best** Italian **coffee** in London. **Creamy, luxurious** and **perfectly blended** with a craftsmanship that is sadly rare in the breakneck pace of city life. Hordes of London's Italian community congregate here to aleviate moments of homesickness by eating vatloads of freshly baked pastries and arguing loudly with the waiters. And if Calcio is your thing, things get enjoyably feisty every Saturday evening, when a Serie A game is screened.

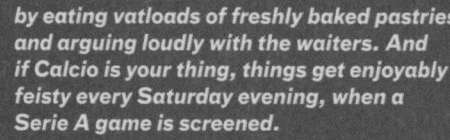

FARRINGDON

Sfizio
35-37 Theobald's Road
WC1X 8SP
020 7831 1888
www.sfizio.co.uk

When this conversation is normal, you know you're not in your average tailors.

Bayode and Claire Oduwole aren't your average tailors. Choose from one of their hundreds of templates, have it altered to fit, and there you are with, as Bayode says, "Neapolitan construction, American stylish and English cuts". Or if you prefer, Mae West meets Mao Tse Tung.

Pokit
53 Lamb's Conduit Street
WC1N 3NB
020 7430 9782

SPANISH

CHORIZO

VEG. SOU

OUTH
ET E.C

How do you condense one of London's most vibrant and hip 'hoods into two pages?

Like this:

Start off at the Farringdon Road end where **Dollar** is the home of 'grills and martinis' and does a pretty fine steak burger. There's also the daily collection of lunchtime stalls providing a light lunch of crepes, Italian sausage or burritos. On the left is the laidback **Al's Café**, here since long before the neighbourhood boomed, and the very height of slow and aloof service.

The **Exmouth Arms** offers a proper English pub atmosphere, and a view of **Brindisa**, the delightful Spanish deli across the road. **Brill** combines CD browsing and damn fine cups of coffee, while a few doors down, the Portuguese **Cafe Kick** is jammed full of table footballers and boozy spectators.

There's global dining worthy of a mention too: **Santore**, with proper Italian cooking (and Italian-

Coffee
Bagels
+Free Wi-Fi
t in/Take Away

paced service too); **Cottons**, the Caribbean joint where you can dance off your indulgences in the downstairs late-night bar; **Moro**, the stylish and modern Moroccan eatery; **Medcalf**, where you can dine or enjoy a drink while taking in their latest exhibition, and the traditional **Clark's** pie-and-mash shop.

Exmouth Market is oh-so-happening that you can even experience that Lower East Side vibe at the more prosaic outlets: the enthusiastic horticulturalists running plant store **Pod**, the bohemian **Metropolitan Books** and the Bill Gates 'Dress-down Friday' feel at **Green Light Pharmacy**.

Even the ubiquitous Starbucks is flanked by the swanky **Sweet** cafe/patisserie and the up-market **Tokum**, which confidently claims to be 'baker, grocer, deli, café'.

You could round off your trip with a more permanent souvenir at the intimidatingly hip (but scrupulously clean) **Family Business** tattoo parlour, though if that is too extreme, **EC One** jewellers offers an array of handmade, award-winning gems.

Exmouth Market
off Rosebery Avenue
EC1R

There are lots of reasons to love the Quality Chophouse. The dark wooden booths and frosted-glass screens; the signs outside that read 'London's Noted Cup Of Tea' and 'Civility'; the waiters so smooth they could be coated in Vaseline. But if there's one reason above all the rest that explains why we love the place, it's the Martin Johnson breakfast:

28-day matured Scottish sirloin steak

Black pudding

A rugby ball of bubble and squeak

Welsh lamb chop

Cumberland sausage

Honey-roasted ham

Tea/coffee, juice and toast

Poached free-range egg

Respect.

The Quality Chophouse
94 Farringdon Road EC1R 3EA
020 7837 5093
www.qualitychophouse.co.uk
Mon-Fri 11.00am-11.30pm, Sat 6.00pm-11.30pm, Sun 12.00pm-11.30pm

Design junkies and gourmets look away. There is nothing for you here.

If, however, you **love** a bit of tack, welcome to _Tinseltown_. It looks like an underground car park that's been decorated by a serial stalker with a fetish for Hollywood. Every minute or so, a deafening 'birthday' klaxon goes off and all the screens switch to a video cavalcade of frankly bemused **celebs** (50 Cent, Xtina, Snoop) giving props to "Yo Tinseltown". In fact it's all rather like the physical embodiment of a 14-year-old girl's Myspace page. But forget all that, even forget the generic fast food. We're here for the milkshakes. Scorning their lightweight competitors **who** think that putting Maltesers in a milkshake is somehow radical, staff at Tinseltown go the whole hog. Name something sweet, and they'll **liquidise** it and stick it in a frosted glass. Pictured here is a cherry Bakewell tart and ice-cream milkshake. With rich toffee sauce. And whipped cream. And chopped nuts. It probably contains the recommended daily calories for **an adult horse** and it makes your teeth itch. But it does taste amazing.

Tinseltown
44-46 St John St
EC1M 4DF
020 7689 2424
Open 24 hours a day, seven days a week

THEY SAY YOU NEVER FORGET YOUR FIRST TIME

Past the tourists and hawkers of the London Dungeon, down a neon-lit underpass, every third car a dodgy minicab, counting the arches till "I think it's this one". Through a nondescript doorway and then the space opens up to room after room. Deep under the rumbles of Waterloo station people are chatting in an abandoned van, their faces lit by neon tubes. A dark velvet-coloured tunnel leads to a wall filled with scratchy paintings, while a circle of torch-lit faces are turned towards a dance piece in a back room. Drinking, discussing, dancing. Every time you go back, <u>Shunt</u>'s reinvented itself. It's a members' club, it's a circus, it's a gallery. It's a theatre, it's a lounge, it's a concert hall.

IT'S AN ADVENTURE

Shunt
Joiner Street
SE1
Wed-Fri, 6pm-11pm
Sat, 8pm-11pm

SATURDAY MORNING
AND THE QUEUE'S
ALREADY FORMING

Inside, people are browsing this temple of cheese, but we're out here in the cold because in a few minutes we'll reach the front of the queue and be able to savour the main event: Grilled Montgomery Cheddar, spring onion and leeks on a sourdough bread.

ELEPHANT
AND CASTLE

Despite its exotic sounding name, anyone who's seen the place would find it hard to imagine that this dumping ground for concrete and bad architecture might contain, hidden away under a railway arch, one of the best clubs in the city. No, not the Ministry of Sound but the very antithesis of that over-priced tourist trap: <u>Corsica Studios</u>.

A throwback to the days when clubs were held in gyms or naughtily appropriated offices, Corsica simply provides a good space in which to listen to very good, very loud music, and in all probability wake up naked on your living room floor two days later with vague memories of good times and random text messages from people you don't know and embarrassing photos on Facebook of you wobbling about on top of a speaker stack wearing a wig.

With its killer sound system, excellent booking policy and, thanks to the out-of-the-way location, a genuinely up-for-it, friendly and musically literate crowd, you'll be hard pressed to find a better place to dance the night away.

Just round the corner from the market is a little London oddity. From the wire fence of an empty car park fly hundreds of tiny ribbons. It's the site of an

UNCONSECRATED GRAVEYARD

used to bury prostitutes from medieval times to the 1850s. After it was dug up as part of the Jubilee Line extension, local people have made it a kind of unofficial blue plaque site, honouring the dead with flowers, ribbons and poetry. There's still a battle going on over how the land will be used but for now there's a little bit of London history hanging from a Borough car-park fence.

Cross Bones Graveyard
Redcross Way
SE1

London doesn't have many culinary claims to fame, but

WE DO MAKE THE BEST

BUBBLE& SQUEAK IN THE WORLD

And the best bubble in London? Maria's. First she was round the corner on Park Street – a Borough institution – then in a cupboard-sized space on Stoney Street, but in her latest location, an unassuming little shed among the shouts and bustle of Borough Market, Maria is in her element. Two steaming pans of potato and cabbage are always on the go for the constant stream of hungry shoppers and traders – most of whom are regulars. It's best on a cold winter's morning. Get there before the 10am crowds, warm up with a cup of three-sugars-please tea and then tuck in to Maria's culinary masterpiece: the bubble, cheese and bacon roll.

Maria's
Borough Market
Stoney Street
SE1 9AA
Weds-Sat

POW!

ROLL UP FOR UNDERGROUND WRESTLING, FILTHY CIRCUS TURNS AND LONDON'S LEAST LIKELY NIGHT OUT

Watch Jack Nicholson
Drink Jack Daniels
ROXY
BAR&
SCREEN
Roxy Bar and Screen
128-132 Borough High Street
SE1 1LB
www.roxybarandscreen.com

Whether nestled in the basement of an independent bookshop or café, among a plethora of picnickers in Golders Green Park or in seasoned comedy critic Bruce Dessau's living room, <u>Laughter In Odd Places</u> is, without a doubt, comedic convention's counterpart.

Stand-ups, sketch acts and storytellers take to unusual stages across the city, each with the shared belief that live comedy needn't be housed in the badly-lit, sticky-floored back room of your average local. The offbeat ethos is reflected in genuinely innovative, exciting material, spearheaded by creator and MC Terry Saunders. Attempting to do for charity shops and museums what anti-folk pioneer Jeffrey Lewis did for New York laundrettes, he also ensures tea-filled flasks and biscuits are on standby for the all-important intervals. To keep track of the next secret location, register at www.laughterinoddplaces.com – the shows' whereabouts and acts might be unpredictable, but the whimsical and welcoming atmosphere awaiting you is an absolute certainty.

Laughter In Odd Places
www.laughterinoddplaces.com

Take at least two knitting needles per person

Mix with various yarns and threads to taste

Apply alcoholic beverages as required

Add 20-50 people of any age

Pour into any available public space – floating bars, underground carriages – wherever will hold the ingredients

Leave for 3-4 hours

Wear when ready

Stitch 'n' Bitch
www.stitchnbitch.co.uk

One fine morning in 1651 three amateur fishermen set off along the River Lea to walk, talk and fish for pike.

Mudlarking. Once the preserve of ragamuffin children and widowed women, it's all about scrabbling in the mud on the shores of the Thames shores, searching for anything of value.

Just beyond the famous Hackney Wick football pitches runs the final stretch of the Lower Lea before it flows into the Thames. Join the river from the Lower Lea Bridge Road and take a walk down past the Springfield Marina, a quiet little community of narrowboat dwellers and boat builders.

Back in the 1850s, the big score was coal fallen from Thames barges, but it was meagre reward for filthy work among banks scattered with dead bodies and detritus.

One of the three was Izaak Walton, soon-to-be author of The Compleat Angler – the first real British fishing book and still in print 350 years later. Here's a river walk dedicated to him.

From here you can join the River Lea by the Middlesex Filter Beds, a remnant of Victorian London but now a nature reserve. Here the Old River Lea can be discovered, surprisingly untouched by industry from the past three centuries. There's meandering path down to the A102 where the 2012 Olympic site begins. It's hardly used and you're more like to come across a heron than another walker.

There are fewer bodies these days, but there's still plenty buried in the silt - pieces of clay pipe, glass bottles (many of them old Bovril bottles, for some reason), bits of old boat and centuries-old pieces of ceramic all turn up regularly.

Lose yourself for a few hours and give silent thought to the three companions who made the same short journey three-and-a-half centuries ago. N.B. An Environment Agency Rod License is needed before fishing the River Lea and no fishing is allowed between March 15th and June 15th.

As you sift, spare a gaze for the gallows outside The Prospect of Whitby, a memorial to the original Execution Dock that was situated outside the Town of Ramsgate pub a bit further along, where pirates, including Captain Kidd, swung. They were left hanging there until three tides had passed over their heads.

Get a mudlarking day permit (£7.50) from the Port of London Authority (01474 562200). Or volunteer for one of environmental charity Thames 21's clean-up programmes, www.thames21.org.uk

For those with piscatorial pursuits in mind, I would recommend a few hours in search of pike. This one-mile stretch of river has been described as "legendary" in the past for the quality of fishing and a still-large head of fish has gives adventurous predators a plentiful meal. They're not the biggest pike you'll ever find but the intense colour and quality is sublime. We recommend a simple technique of wobbling half a mackerel and touch feel for any bites, keep it simple and move on after every two or three casts. A great time to try is early spring with the daffodils and blossom in bloom, or during mid-summer for those lean fighting predatory pike.

You'll need a permit (details above) but mudlarking on the Thames by Wapping at low tide still carries with it an air of smuggling and skulduggery, especially if you can catch a day with overcast skies or a Thames fog.

Pubs to visit afterwards: The Prospect of Whitby (57 Wapping Wall), William Kidd (108 Wapping High Street), the Town of Ramsgate (62 Wapping High Street).

"It's riddled with asbestos and fungus so don't touch anything. I've just found out the electricity's not working, so it's pitch black down there. And shin-deep in water." Andrew Smith of Subterranea Britannica isn't really selling this trip to see a deserted World War II bunker.

We recreate Churchill's only visit here for a War Cabinet meeting (though I doubt many of the people taking part then were holding torches and wearing wellies). Our Churchill is rather more Japanese and significantly gigglier than I imagine the original was, and I get to stand in for Clem Attlee.

We wade through abandoned communications rooms, map rooms and generator rooms. We try to find Churchill's bedroom (after the war, locals would apparently try to entice girls down there to 'see where Churchill slept' – a chat-up line so inept that it makes you yearn for those simpler times). We get wet.

But if you want to explore London's hidden underground spaces, Sub Brit are the people you need. They've got access to more bunkers, mines and abandoned Tube stations than anyone else. And if you ask nicely they'll show you round.

By nine we're soaked, chockfull of history and ready to hit the surface. Two people behind me are already planning a trip to see the catacombs of Istanbul...

Such as this trip to an abandoned bunker, designed as a Luftwaffe-safe Government headquarters in the forties, and now sitting mouldering under a row of suburban homes. However you feel about being wet, dark and exposed to toxic chemicals, there's something about the Sub Brit guides' knowledge and enthusiasm that is infectious.

Is Earlham Street the geekiest street in London?

COVENT GARDEN

Dungeons and Dragons fiends haunt the Orc's Nest, while strange art people crowd that little shop that only sells book upon book of royalty-free images. Trainer geeks come from the world over for the Adidas store. And design geeks all head for Magma.

Every spare bit of space in Magma is packed with hard-to-find fashion mags, strange books on Japanese cartoons, NY punk stuff and.. well... y'know, cool stuff for people with Apple Macs. A few doors down, they've opened a place selling designer toys, games and jewellery. Never have credit cards received such a nerdy bashing.

Magma
8 & 16 Earlham Street
WC2H 9RY
020 7240 8498

This is what Americans expect London to look like.

Tucked down one of those little streets that run from the Strand to the river, Gordon's is almost comically old-time Londonish. The entrance is down a rickety, unmarked set of wooden stairs. Inside it's varying shades of brown, covered with ten generations of dusty pictures, torn posters and general knick-knackery. The wines are great (and by the glass), the staff are unflustered (and surprisingly hot) and there's a long row of tables outside for those two weeks we call the British summer.

Get here early – it's best before 3.30pm, after which it fills with suits, and the staff are too busy to think about the best wine to go with the excellent cheese plate.

Gordon's Wine Bar
47 Villiers St
WC2N

Some thoughts by Paul Jones, gallery founder...

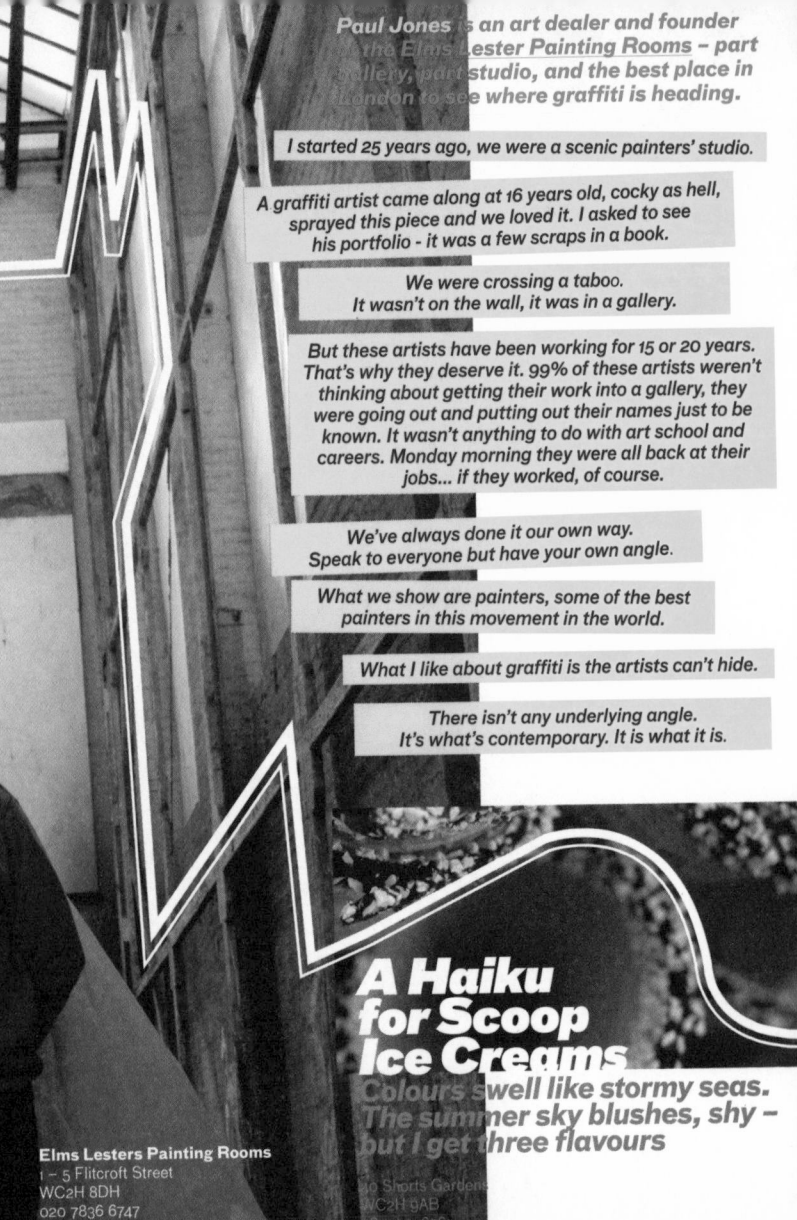

Paul Jones is an art dealer and founder
the Elms Lester Painting Rooms – part
gallery, part studio, and the best place in
London to see where graffiti is heading.

I started 25 years ago, we were a scenic painters' studio.

A graffiti artist came along at 16 years old, cocky as hell,
sprayed this piece and we loved it. I asked to see
his portfolio - it was a few scraps in a book.

We were crossing a taboo.
It wasn't on the wall, it was in a gallery.

But these artists have been working for 15 or 20 years.
That's why they deserve it. 99% of these artists weren't
thinking about getting their work into a gallery, they
were going out and putting out their names just to be
known. It wasn't anything to do with art school and
careers. Monday morning they were all back at their
jobs... if they worked, of course.

We've always done it our own way.
Speak to everyone but have your own angle.

What we show are painters, some of the best
painters in this movement in the world.

What I like about graffiti is the artists can't hide.

There isn't any underlying angle.
It's what's contemporary. It is what it is.

A Haiku for Scoop Ice Creams

Colours swell like stormy seas.
The summer sky blushes, shy –
but I get three flavours

Elms Lesters Painting Rooms
1 – 5 Flitcroft Street
WC2H 8DH
020 7836 6747
www.elmslesters.co.uk

40 Shorts Gardens
WC2H 9AB
0871 971 6261

Monmouth Street Coffee

No mobile phones.
No gimmicky flavours.
No memorabilia.
No chain.
No problem.

Monmouth Street Coffee
27 Monmouth Street
WC2H 9EU
020 7379 3516

Camp as Christmas,

sprinkled with bar staff in angel wings and packed with after-work cocktailers, there's no way you could describe the _Cellar Door_ as sophisticated. It's set in a converted underground toilet, for a start. Expect rowdy Abba singalongs, ties getting loosened, snogging, shouting and people disappearing off with unsuitable others.

Cellar Door
Zero Aldwych
WC2R 0HT
020 7240 8848

Downstairs is great obviously – the best photographic exhibitions in the city, a bookshop that you pop in to for a postcard and leave two hours later with a credit card bill that'll have your head spinning, and a damn fine cup of coffee in the cafeteria. Upstairs is the print sales room, a lesser-known treasure where you can browse through some of the 20th and 21st century's best images, and even, if you're feeling a bit flash, treat yourself to a small slice of history.

Photographers' Gallery
5 & 8 Great Newport Street
WC2H 7HY
020 7831 1772
www.photonet.org.uk

The Africa Centre

For some it's a politics thing – a place that keeps African issues in the capital's mind. For some it's a cultural gateway. But for most Londoners it's the place where Soul II Soul threw the best parties in a generation. Sweaty, raucous all-back-to-mine parties. Fela Kuti and the Fun Boy Three. Cross The Tracks and Keep On Movin'. A Happy Face A Thumpin' Bass For A Lovin' Race!

38 King Street
WC2E 8JT
020 7836 1973

They run a shop full of printing booths on Endell Street. We asked Hunter what it was all about. "The shop is called _Flora Print Club_. We are currently doing Japanese photo stickers and various printing on t-shirts, cups, tiles and puzzles. In the Far East, people fancy the lovely pics and pink style things, and printing these lovely stickers is an expression of love, love between couple and love between friends.

This is Hunter-Li. And Connie Chan.

I opened this shop because I think London is a fashion city, it has the soil to let various trendy things grow. People should have a try to experience some new fun, many thanks."

Flora Print Club
Endell Street
WC2
Seven days a week
2pm-8pm

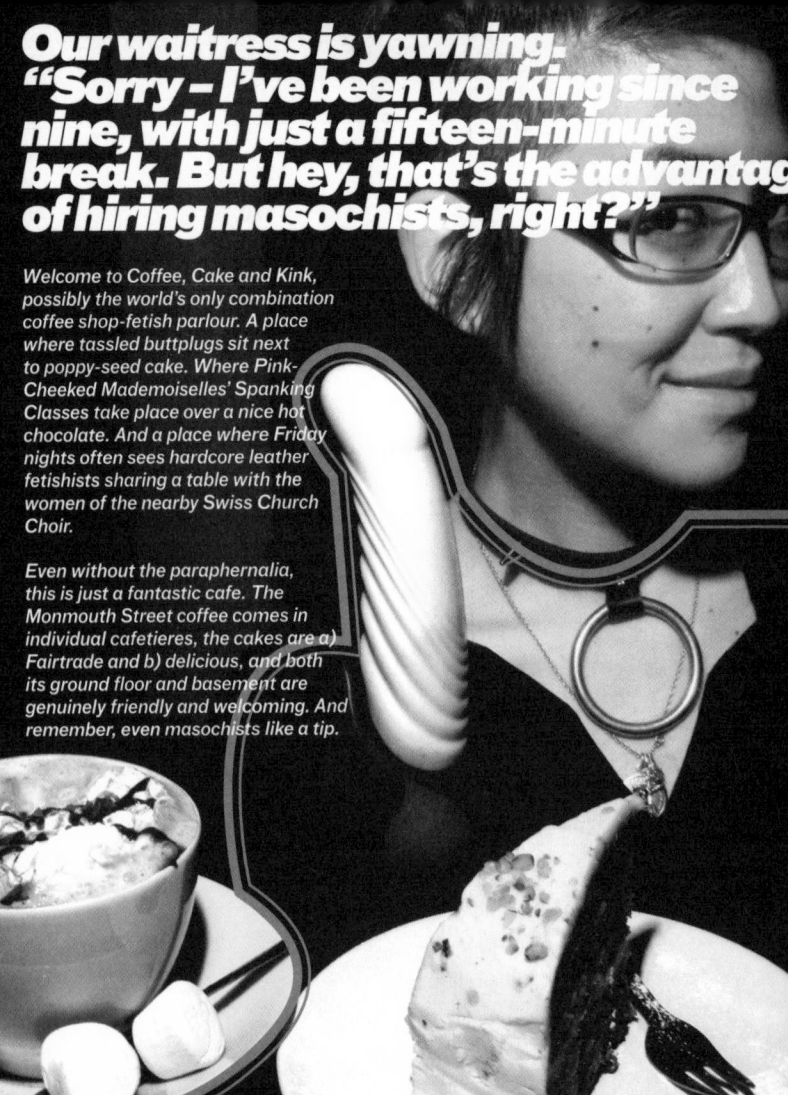

Our waitress is yawning. "Sorry – I've been working since nine, with just a fifteen-minute break. But hey, that's the advantage of hiring masochists, right?"

Welcome to Coffee, Cake and Kink, possibly the world's only combination coffee shop-fetish parlour. A place where tassled buttplugs sit next to poppy-seed cake. Where Pink-Cheeked Mademoiselles' Spanking Classes take place over a nice hot chocolate. And a place where Friday nights often sees hardcore leather fetishists sharing a table with the women of the nearby Swiss Church Choir.

Even without the paraphernalia, this is just a fantastic cafe. The Monmouth Street coffee comes in individual cafetieres, the cakes are a) Fairtrade and b) delicious, and both its ground floor and basement are genuinely friendly and welcoming. And remember, even masochists like a tip.

Coffee, Cake and Kink
61 Endell Street
WC2H 9AJ
020 7419 2996
www.coffeecakeandkink.com
Mon-Thur 11am-8pm, Fri & Sat 11am-11pm, Sun 11am-8pm

Alana, co-owner of Coffee, Cake and Kink once compiled a fetish map of London. Here are the highlights.

Shops

1) Fairy Goth Mother Knows her corsets

2) Fettered Pleasures For all your gimp suit and mask needs

3) Liberation Great latex catsuits just round the corner from Coffee, Cake and Kink

4) House of Harlot For latex and leather couture

5) Honour For shiny PVC

6) London Fetish Fair and LAM Two great days out on a Sunday if you like markets

7) Regulation Great for gay rubber lovers

8) Expectations Gay fetish shop, very underground

9) Rob of London Kinky gay shop for when you're fed up with M&S. Near Oxford Street

0) Sh! The first women-only sex shop in the UK

Clubs

1) Subversion - Play and dance club

2) Torture Garden - Play and dance club

3) Club Rub - Themed fetish parties every month

4) Back Street - A gay S&M club, literally down a back street in Mile End

5) Hoist - Gay leather and rubber club in Vauxhall

Treadwell's is like the corner shop for any self-respecting London esotericist

White witches drop in for virgin beeswax candles and hand-carved druid wands before popping downstairs to catch a talk on 'Mesopotamian Magic for Bending the King's Ear'. Sorcerers pick up pristine copies of The Tiruvaimoli of Nammalvar while Vampyrs flick through Dark Nights fanzine and lust after rowan-handled knives. Historians pass the time before their 'Czech Ethnography of Spirits, Witches and Gods' lecture by flicking through de Quincey's 'Confessions of an English Opium Eater' – written next door. All in all, a friendly little community, making Treadwell's one of the happiest bookshops in the capital. The staff are relentlessly cheerful and well-read, browsing and reading is positively encouraged – there's an always-occupied 'Browser's Sofa' – and other shoppers happily come up and chat about your purchases. They also do a nice line in Wiccan greeting cards.

Treadwell's
34 Tavistock Street
020 7240 8906
12pm-7pm every day

Fig. 1

Mayfair

Stephen Wiltshire Gallery
www.stephenwiltshire.co.uk
5 Royal Opera Arcade
Pall Mall

Churchill Hou...

...h Giraldas 160/. 1311

...e Balkans "/. 134

166

...h Giraldas 160/. 166

...midad Perlas 90/. 166

...e Giraldas 160/

...midad P...

...e Balka...

SW1A 1ES
020 7930 3787

Fortnum and Mason

Yes, the Queen shops there (or someone shops for her – she probably doesn't push her own trolley. Yes, it stocks things like quail's eggs and Gentleman's Relish. Yes, it was founded on the proceeds from selling the royal family's discarded candles. But for one thing and one thing only should the name of Fortnum and Mason be revered: it was here, in 1738, that the scotch egg was invented. So next time you're unwrapping one of those little beauties in the harsh glare of a petrol station forecourt at 4am, give silent thanks to the emporium of Hugh Mason and William Fortnum. (And yes, they still sell 'em. But for a real gourmet egg, we recommend the huge version on sale at the Norfolk Arms in Fitzrovia.)

181 Piccadilly
W1A 1ER
020 7734 8040

Fig. II

Fig. III

Fig I ~ Stephen Wiltshire Gallery

Not many artists have a London gallery to themselves. Halfway down
London's oldest shopping arcade sits the <u>Stephen Wiltshire Gallery</u>,
dedicated to the work of an autistic genius. You might have seen him on
TV: 1987's "Foolish Wise Ones" and 2001's "Fragments of Genius" looked
at Stephen's uncanny ability to capture complex scenes and cityscapes
from just one viewing. Go up the tiny winding staircase in the shop
and you'll find the walls covered with his impossibly detailed drawings,
with New York street scenes, huge-scale city drawings and newer,
more abstract work. Downstairs is the studio. A couple of days a week,
Stephen himself is there, working away with his family around him. Not
your usual gallery at all.

Fig II ~ JJ Fox & Robert Lewis

Wistful smokers should make a beeline for <u>JJ Fox & Robert Lewis</u>,
London's last word in cigars and smoking accoutrements. Walk into the
humidor – set at the exact temperature and humidity of Cuba – and then
sneak downstairs for a gander at their wonderful museum. Oscar Wilde still
owes them money, and Winnie Churchill's ordering chair is surprisingly
comfortable, although I'm fairly sure I shouldn't have sat in it. Tant pis.

Fig III – James Lock

Stop off in Berry Brothers for a spot of Dutch courage at one of their
whisky tastings and clock just how many limbs you'd have to flog to buy
a bottle of Petrus. A few doors up, it's London's premier hatters, <u>James
Lock</u>. No Philip Treacy millinery here, this is quality toppers, ski hats
and riding wear plus the obligatory viewblockers for weddings. Check
out Nelson's hat hanging on the wall, the old order slips from famous
customers and see what properly made hats look like when they don't
have all manner of clutter on them.

Fig IV ~ John Lobb

Up the road from James Lock is this ancient oasis of discretion and jawdropping craftsmanship. The current cobbling <u>Lobb</u>, William, bustles around in an apron and is manners itself. A pair of custom-made brogues will set you back nearly £2000; while chewing on that thought, have a look at their display of shoes, and watch footwear being crafted through a squillion different stages in the workshop.

Fig V ~ DR Harris & Company

<u>DR Harris & Co</u> is one of those traditional chemists you think have disappeared for good. While they've sadly stopped stocking their legendary hangover cures, there are enough curiosities in here, as well as the tedious necessities of modern life, to thrill the most pharmaceutical magpie. Vintage devotees flock here for hair and skin care.

Fig VI ~ Truefitt and Hill

Across the road is the world's oldest barber shop, <u>Truefitt and Hill</u>. Sod Trumpers – you terrible tourist! – this is the real deal. Their marketing manager is called Graham Barber, which is almost too brilliant. Treat yourself to a proper haircut (around £50) and soak in the propriety and peace of the place.

Fig VII ~ Postcard Teas

It's a surprise to find any kind of bargain on New Bond Street, let alone London's best cup of tea for a princely £1.50. But <u>Postcard Teas</u> isn't your average kind of place. Brainchild of tea-lover extraordinaire, traveller and all-round good egg Timothy d'Offay, this tiny shop is home to all manner of rare teas from your oolongs to your chais. If you get Timothy himself serving you (and you might – it's that kind of place) then it's a little like being guided by a tea sommelier. Pick a good 'un and you can even send it off as a gift – the shop has its own postbox.

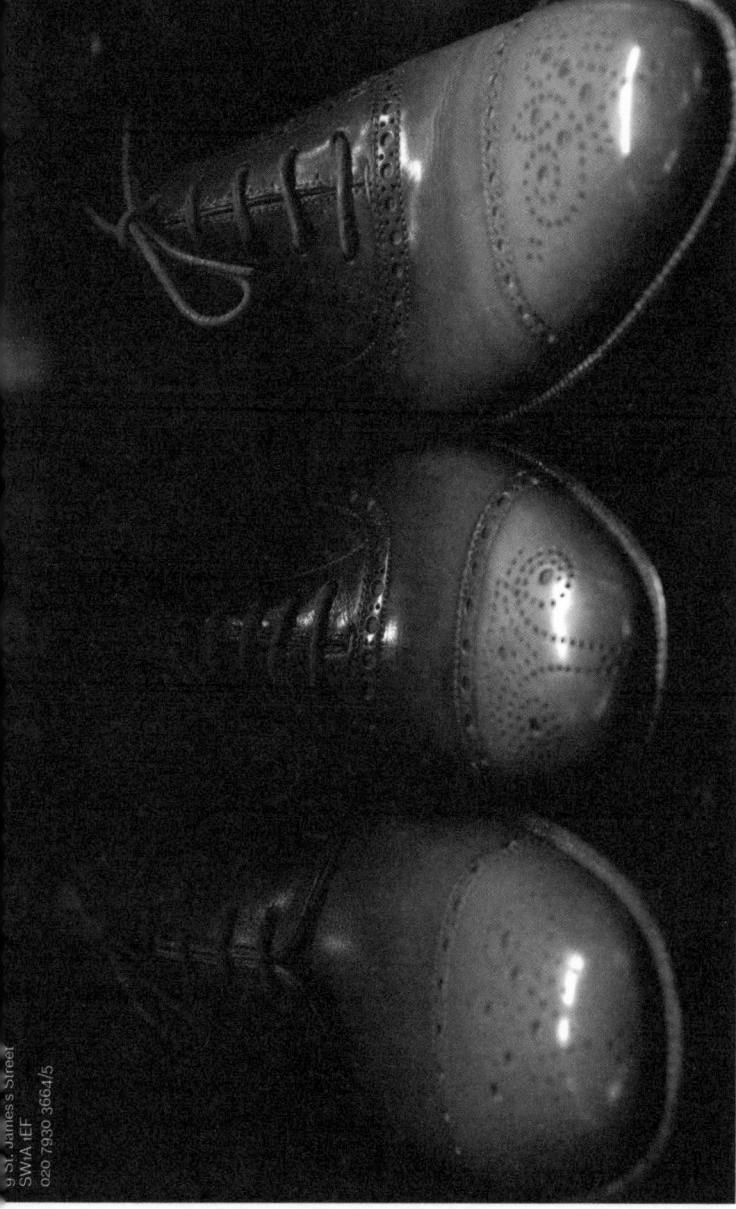

Fig. IV

Fig. V

Fig. VI

D.R.HARRIS & Co. Lᵈ
ESTABLISHED 1790

BY APPOINTMENT
TO H.M. QUEEN ELIZABETH
THE QUEEN MOTHER
CHEMISTS

The Original
PICK-ME-UP

D.R. Harris

D. R. HARRIS & CO. LTD. 29 ST. JAMES'S STREET. LONDON SW

ROSEMARY & THYME

LIMME

D R Harris and Co
29 St. James's Street
SW1A 1HB

Truefitt & Hill
71 St. James's Street
SW1A 1PH

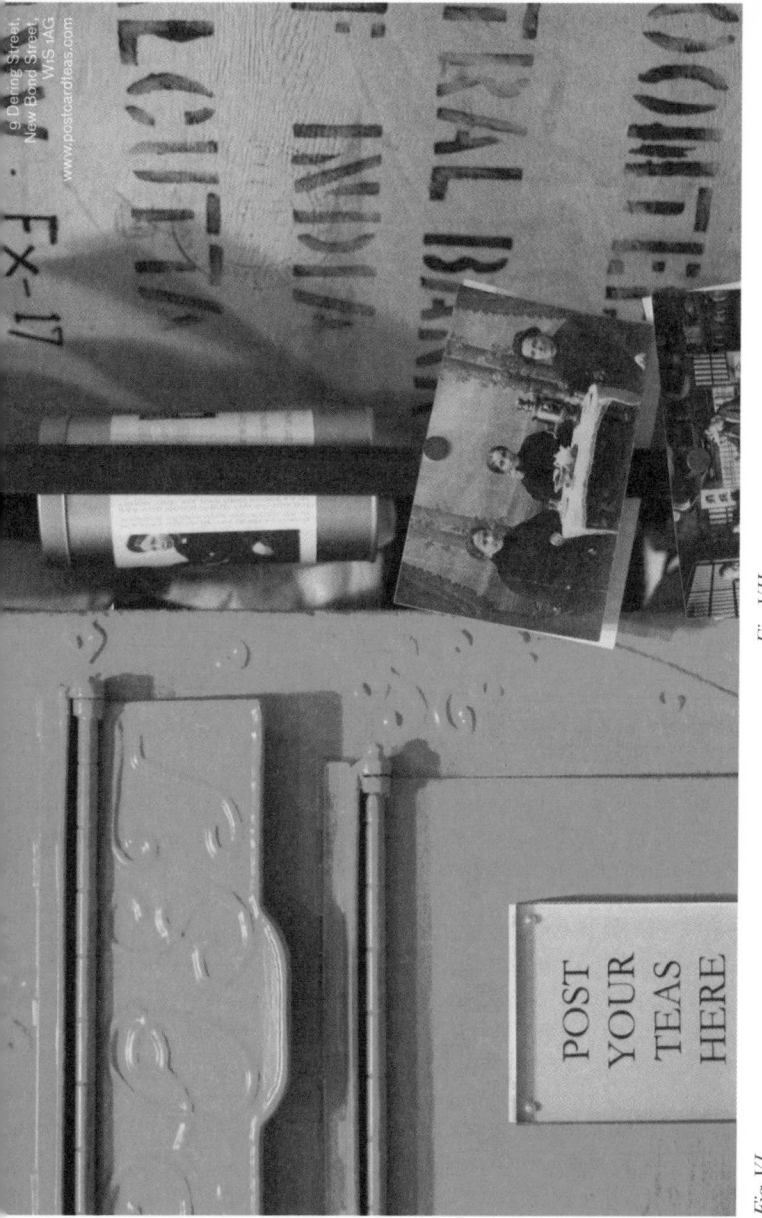

POST
YOUR
TEAS
HERE

Fig. VI

Fig. VII

BY FAR THE LONGEST, MOST BEGUILING AND BEST KNOWN OF LONDON'S TANGLE OF A DOZEN-OR-SO SUBTERRANEAN THAMES TRIBUTARIES IS THE FIVE-MILE-LONG FLEET RIVER. THERE IS A BAF- FLING ARRAY OF GUIDES CHARTING ITS WINDING UNDERGROUND COURSE, MOST OF THEM TAK- EN UP IN TEDIOUS TOPOGRAPHICAL DETAIL WITH OFTEN CONTRADICTORY DIRECTIONS. HOWEV- ER, IN MUCH THE SAME WAY THAT "WHY DON'T YOU?" INSTRUCTED VIEWERS TO TURN OFF THEIR TELEVISION SETS AND GO AND DO SOMETHING LESS BORING INSTEAD, LE COOL READERS ARE ADVISED TO CHUCK AWAY THEIR GUIDEBOOK (LEAVING IT IN A SAFE PLACE FOR EASY FUTURE REFERENCE), DON THEIR PSYCHOGEOGRAPHI- CAL DEERSTALKERS AND HUNT OUT THE ROUTE FOR THEMSELVES. THE CLUES ARE MANY AND OF- TEN OBVIOUS – STREET NAMES LIKE FLEET ROAD AND ANGLER'S LANE GIVE THE GAME AWAY WHILE THE LONDON LANDSCAPE IS CONSPICUOUSLY MOULDED BY ITS ANCIENT CONDUIT. SPOT AN ODD CURVE IN THE ROAD AND CHANCES ARE A RIVER ONCE RAN THROUGH IT. IF IT'S RAINING, EVEN

THE PUDDLES CAN OFFER A HINT AS TO THE MOST LIKELY DIRECTION OF THE WATER BELOW. THE RIVER CAN OCCASIONALLY BE GLIMPSED RUNNING FAR BELOW THE SURFACE THROUGH GRATINGS, SUCH AS THOSE IN THE MIDDLE OF FLEET ROAD, WHILE THE PIPED EASTERN FORK BRIEFLY POPS UP ABOVE GROUND TO CROSS A RAILWAY LINE NEAR DARTMOUTH PARK, LIKE A HUGE IRON WORM. THE FLEET BEGINS IN THE SERIES OF PONDS STRADDLING EITHER SIDE OF HAMPSTEAD HEATH, ITS TWO MAIN FORKS CONVERGING CLOSE TO KENTISH TOWN – WHOSE NAME MAY BE A CORRUPTION OF KEN DITCH, REFERRING TO KENWOOD HOUSE ON THE HEATH. IT MEANDERS BENEATH THE BACK STREETS OF CAMDEN AND KING'S CROSS – WHICH, WHEN KNOWN AS BATTLE BRIDGE, WAS THE SITE OF BOUDICA'S LAST STAND AGAINST THE ROMANS – SWINGING ROUND THE FORMER RUBBISH DUMP MOUNT PLEASANT BEFORE CUTTING THE VERY VISIBLE FLEET VALLEY DOWN FARRINGDON ROAD. IT FINALLY JOINS THE THAMES VIA A HATCH BENEATH BLACKFRIARS BRIDGE, WHICH CAN STILL BE SEEN AT LOW TIDE.

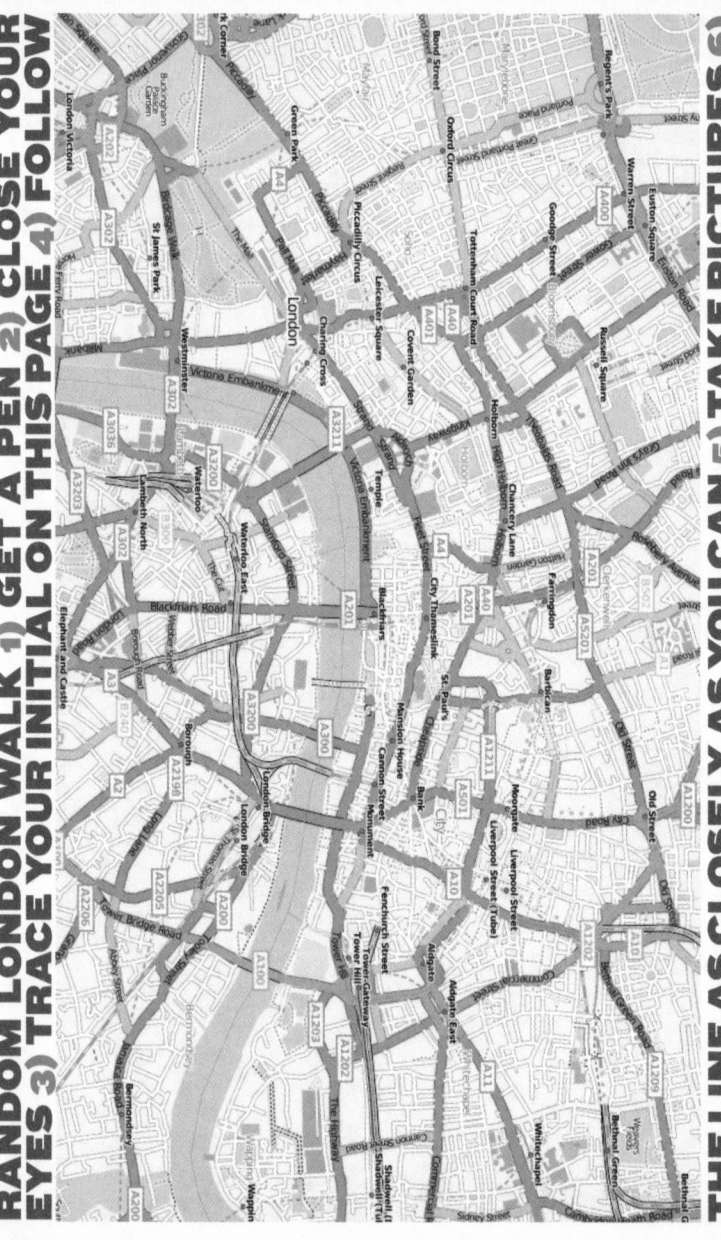

RANDOM LONDON WALK 1) GET A PEN 2) CLOSE YOUR EYES 3) TRACE YOUR INITIAL ON THIS PAGE 4) FOLLOW

THE LINE AS CLOSELY AS YOU CAN 5) TAKE PICTURES 6) LET US KNOW HOW YOU GOT ON. LONDON@LECOOL.COM

THE CAPITAL RING: MOST LONDONERS WILL BE AT LEAST VAGUELY AWARE OF THE LONDON LOOP, A 150-MILE PEDESTRIAN CIRCUMNAVIGATION OF GREATER LONDON, POPULARLY KNOWN AS THE "WALKER'S M25". LESS WELL KNOWN IS THE LOOP'S LITTLE BROTHER, THE CAPITAL RING. IT'S A 78-MILE CIRCUIT ROUGHLY TRACING THE BORDER OF ZONES 2 AND 3. WHEREAS THE LOOP IS PRINCIPALLY THE DOMAIN OF THE HIGHLY INTREPID OR FOOLHARDY, NECESSITATING HOURS OF PLANNING AND HUNDREDS OF POUNDS' WORTH OF HIKING BOOTS, WATERPROOFS, MAPS AND COMPASSES, THE BEAUTY OF THE CAPITAL RING IS THAT ANYONE WITH TWO REASONABLY FUNCTIONING LOWER LIMBS CAN TACKLE IT EASILY. ALL YOU NEED IS AN OYSTER CARD - TO GET TO AND FROM YOUR START AND FINISH POINTS - AND A DECENT PAIR OF TRAINERS. THE WHOLE ROUTE IS CLEARLY SIGNPOSTED WITH LIME GREEN CAPITAL RING ARROWS, SO IT'S EASILY DOABLE WITHOUT MAPS, ALTHOUGH AN A-TO-Z IS PROBABLY A GOOD IDEA FOR THE PARTS WHERE THE LOCAL VANDALS HAVE HAD A BIT OF FUN OBSCURING THE ROUTE MARKERS. IT'S DIVIDED INTO 15 HANDY CHUNKS OF BETWEEN THREE AND SEVEN MILES, BUT YOU CAN HOP ON AND OFF WHEREVER YOU FANCY, AS IT'S NEATLY DESIGNED TO NEVER BE MORE THAN A COUPLE OF MILES FROM A TUBE, TRAM OR RAILWAY STATION, MAKING CLEVER USE OF CANAL TOWPATHS, PUBLIC PARKS, CEMETERIES, RESERVOIRS, NATURE RESERVES AND OTHER GREEN SPACES, AT TIMES IT'S ALMOST IMPOSSIBLE TO BELIEVE YOU ARE EXPLORING ONE OF THE WORLD'S MOST DENSELY POPULATED METROPOLISES. ITS HIGHLIGHTS ARE MANY AND VARIED - RICHMOND PARK, THE PLAYING FIELDS OF HARROW, THE WOOLWICH TUNNEL, ELTHAM PALACE, SHOOTER'S HILL... BUT THE REAL JOY IS IN DISCOVERING PARTS OF THE CITY YOU WOULD PROBABLY NEVER OTHERWISE VISIT. THE DUPLICITOUSLY-NAMED GREENWAY - RESEMBLING A DISUSED RAILWAY LINE, BUT ACTUALLY A VICTORIAN SEWER TRAVERSING EAST LONDON - MAY NOT BE ONE OF THE MOST ATTRACTIVE SIGHTS, BUT ITS POST-APOCALYPTIC AMBIENCE HAS A STRANGE BEAUTY ALL OF ITS OWN. THE REST WE'LL LEAVE YOU TO DISCOVER FOR YOURSELF. GOOGLE IT FOR DETAILED ROUTE INFORMATION ON THE TFL SITE, OR BUY "THE OFFICIAL GUIDEBOOK TO THE CAPITAL RING" PUBLISHED BY AURUM PRESS, £12.99

26-28 WHITFIELD STREET
020 7631 0088

You can usually tell the newcomers at <u>Crazy Bear</u>. They fill up on cocktails. They chill out in the leather-lined booths. They go to the toilet. They freak out. Quite how wise it is to install a bathroom that's mirrored on every surface, in an establishment dedicated to the pursuit of inebriation, is a question for the ages... but most people come back enough times to get used to peeing in a hall of mirrors.

That's cos Crazy Bear, for all its cocktail-bar swankiness, is a proper old-fashioned local. Tucked away down a Fitzrovia sidestreet, it's packed with well-heeled locals and staff that know a good thing when they see one. The Thai food upstairs is good, the drinks downstairs are better, and there's that air of where-everybody-knows-your-name-ness that makes you want to move in round the corner.

CRAZY BEAR
WWW.CRAZYBEARGROUP.CO.UK

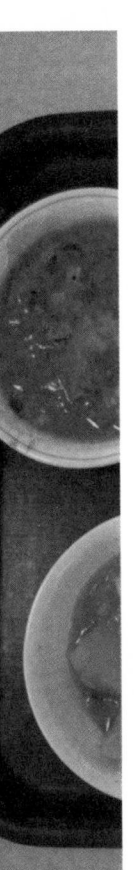

41 Fitzroy Square
020 7387 0411

Plain Rice - £1.20
Dahl - £1
Vegetable Curry - £1.40
Fish Curry - £2.30
Poppadum - 20p

Lunch for two, looking onto one of
London's most charming squares - £6.10
Don't expect waiters, booze or tablecloths.
Just a decent Indian lunch for the
price of a couple of cappuccinos on
nearby Charlotte Street.

Indian YMCA
Lunch Mon-Fri 12pm-2pm
and 12.30pm-1.30pm at the weekends.
Dinner 7pm-8.30pm every day
Arrive early for lunch. Monday night is
vegetarian night.

14 BURY PLACE
WC1A 2JL
020 7269 9030

BOOKS
foxed or dog-eared,
usurped by a new paperback edition,
squeezed out by newer and more exciting
rivals for space,
seek new owner happy to pay

HALF- PRICE

Look to your right.

LONDON REVIEW BOOKSHOP
WWW.LRBSHOP.CO.UK

23 RATHBONE STREET
W1T 1NG
020 7636 1127

It was built as a brothel in 1730. The pub opened in
1860. Dylan Thomas and George Orwell drank here.
The pies are amazing. The beer is great. Cheers.

NEWMAN ARMS PUB & PIE ROOM
WWW.NEWMANARMS.CO.UK
MON-FRI 12PM-12AM
PIES 12PM-3PM, 6PM-9PM

105 GREAT RUSSELL STREET
WC1B 3RY

"Kids come in looking for Harry Potter," says the assistant when we ask about the customers in <u>Cornelissen & Son's</u> art supplies shop. And there is a little of the Diagon Alley about this little treasure trove. The jars on the walls may contain thousands of different paints not potions, and the drawers are crammed with handmade pastels rather than wands, but there's still the air of a magical laboratory in the place. It's unashamedly old-fashioned, packed with artists looking for oilbars and paintsticks and alkyd and siccatives, and guaranteed to make you want to be back in art class.

CORNELISSEN & SON'S ART SUPPLIES SHOP

25 Newman St
WiT 1PN
020 7631 3174

The bar is long and thin and cool and a bit different and the first Nordic bar/restaurant to open in London and it's kinda sophisticated during the day and by night it gets rammed and then everyone starts drinking like Scandinavians.

Nordic Bar
www.nordicbar.com
Mon-Wed 11am-11pm,
Thu 11am-11.30pm, Fri 11am-12am,
Sat 6pm-12am

12-13 Wells St
WiT 3PA
020 7323 1228

There's a certain kind of autumn afternoon. When the suns streams in low through the massive stained-glass windows of The Champion. And throws broken bits of light over the tables and the chairs, and the crisp packets and the golden half-pints. When this is the most beautiful place in the city.

The Champion

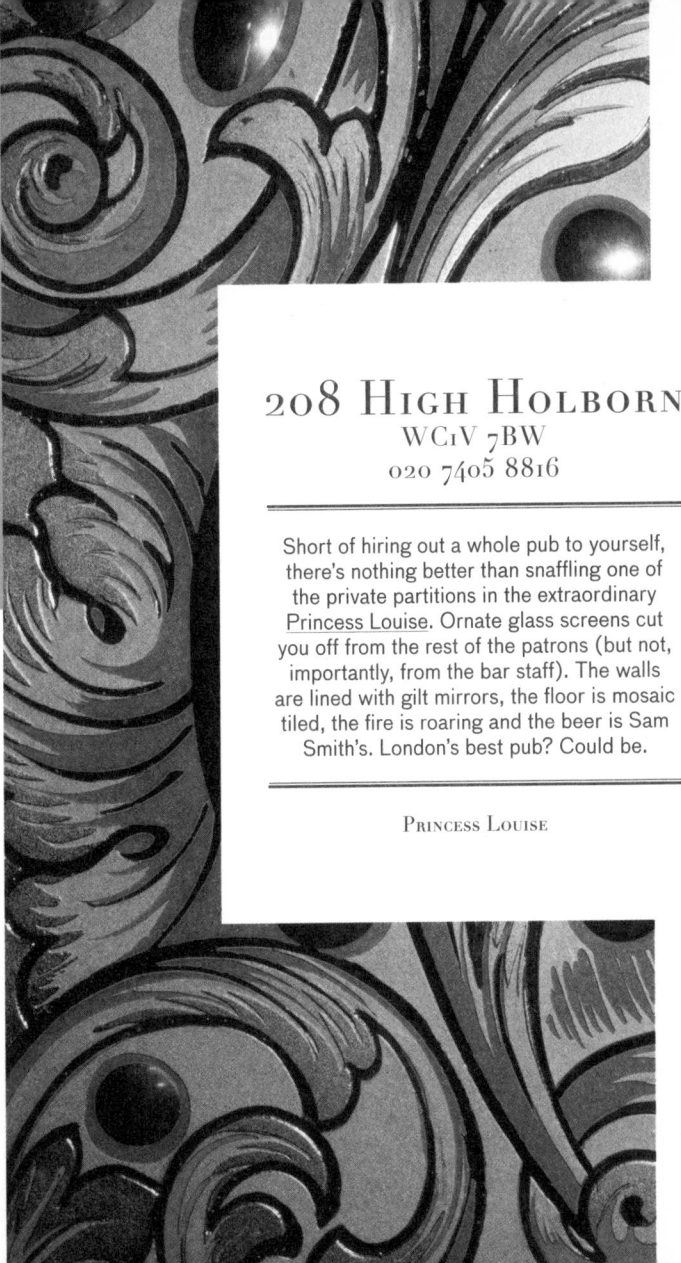

208 High Holborn
WC1V 7BW
020 7405 8816

Short of hiring out a whole pub to yourself, there's nothing better than snaffling one of the private partitions in the extraordinary <u>Princess Louise</u>. Ornate glass screens cut you off from the rest of the patrons (but not, importantly, from the bar staff). The walls are lined with gilt mirrors, the floor is mosaic tiled, the fire is roaring and the beer is Sam Smith's. London's best pub? Could be.

Princess Louise

|ðə last ˈt(y)oōzˌdā səˈsīətē|

Noun

1. *a 'Pataphysical Organisation' that endeavours to further your sense of decadence while exploring the esoteric aspects of London culture through bizarre parties and literary gatherings.*

2. *hist. a place that organises many great balls throughout the year and excellent nights such as 'Loss: an Evening of Exquisite Misery', among others.*

Verb

1. *'To <u>Last Tuesday Society</u>' from 'to party with decadence, among dead partridges suspended from the ceiling'; also from 'to dance to forgotten music wonderfully reproduced by oddly clad DJs while wearing your most sinful outfit'.*

LAST TUESDAY SOCIETY

WWW.THELASTTUESDAYSOCIETY.ORG

BEDFORD WAY
WC1H 9EU
020 7183 1979

It doesn't start well. Down the car-park ramp, round the back of the tired-looking Tavistock Hotel, two likely sorts sat on plastic chairs take your cash and point you to a maze of service corridors that give you that full-on "Hello Cleveland" vibe. And then you're inside, and place is packed. The rockabillies are drinking beer and watching the bands, the students are six-deep at the bar (buy your wine by the bottle to avoid repeat queues), the boys are ten-pin bowling (badly), the girls are doing karaoke (worse) and by midnight, the whole damn lot of them are on the dancefloor. Scruffy, cheap, noisy, flirty – everything you need for a great London night out.

BLOOMSBURY BOWLING

102 DRUMMOND STREET
NW1 2HN
020 7383 0918

This is Antonio. We popped into the <u>African Kitchen Gallery</u> on a rainy afternoon to look at the bits and bobs of art, but the menu looked so good that we asked if it was too early for food. It was, but he said he'd "rustle us up something anyway." Fifteen minutes later he was bringing us sweet potato balls, and spinach and melon seed in palm oil. Twenty minutes later he was extolling the joys of drinking in the afternoon. Twenty-five minutes later he was bringing us steamed Tilapa fish in beans and tomato sauce with jollof rice. Half an hour later he was telling us how to cook Nigerian food. Thirty-five minutes later he was handing us free rice-and-cranberry sweets to be dipped in cocoa, and ginger beer so fearsomely strong that we needed glasses of water straight afterwards. "Tell your friends," said Antonio. Done.

AFRICAN KITCHEN GALLERY
WWW.AFRIKANKITCHEN.COM

28 RATHBONE PLACE
W1T 1JF
020 7636 8228

The trouble with writing this book is that you have to give away some of your secrets. <u>Bourne & Hollingsworth</u> is one of those places. It's everything you wouldn't expect in the West End. Tucked away down in a basement, this tiny speakeasy gin joint lives in the 1920s and the owners have dedicated themselves into getting the best drinks they can. The gin fizzes are ace and the ever-dapper, ever-helpful bar staff will go out of their way to make sure you get something you want. The toilets (if you can find them behind the hidden door) are a treasure trove of flea market trinkets. Depending what night you go, you might find live music or the most stylish of DJs spinning seven-inches in the fireplace, or even stumble into one of their Prohibition nights when the drinks are served in tea cups. Stag dos or big groups of idiots aren't welcome. If you're gonna go, then be cool, you don't want to spoil one of my favourite places.

BOURNE & HOLLINGSWORTH

The best night you never heard of?

club

ve

That's how you heard about it – a word between friends that the cool little hairdressers on the Kentish Town Road was having one of its irregular and infamous parties – all buckets of beer in the back room while the Alabama 3 play live, and top mixologists in the graffiti gallery. It's still pretty much locals-only but check the website – you never know when word will slip out.

Flaxon Ptootch
237 Kentish Town Road
NW5 2JT
www.flaxonptootch.com

Sit in the window seat of the Good Mixer and you'll see 'em wander past. Rockabillies, bikers Mark Lamarr.

Often with an A-Z in their hand. Trying to work out if that concrete shed at the top of Inverness Street can possibly, really be <u>Sounds That Swing</u>. It is. Don't judge a book by its cover – inside is the rockingest, swingingest collection of old 45s, reissues and compilations on their own No Hit label, and general 50s coolness. If it's good enough for the rockabillies (and Lamarr, and Robert Plant) it should be good enough for us.

Sounds That Swing
46 Inverness Street
NW1 7HB,
020 7267 4682
Hours: erm.. let's say 'patchy'. I'd call first.

It looks like a grim shack on a grim road. It is not.

<u>Bintang</u> is the best feature of Kentish Town Road and a chilli-driven stumble from the Abbey pub for afters. The more circumspect enjoy huge helpings of non-spicy noodles, whereas a more caustic mouthful can be found in the range of flaming-hot Ulek specialties, laced with mounds of raw chilli. Eat downstairs in the dark for maximum fairy-light cosiness, or out in the garden during the summer; and bring your own booze. True, ignoring the bare torsos of residents in the neighbouring windows is a challenge. But then, Bintang is a charming shack on a grim road.

Bintang
93 Kentish Town Road
NW1 8NY
020 7813 3393/3392
www.bintangrestaurant.com

Looking for the perfect boozer to drink your little face off in the illustrious CAMDEN TOWN?

With squillions of bars and crowds thicker than the latest cast of Big Brother, Camden can be a doozie of a place to tuck in for a guzzle. Take this quiz to find out which watering hole is built for you.

WHAT IS YOUR PREFERRED BEVERAGE?

a) Shot of Jagermeister, bought by a stranger and drunk straight from a test-tube.

b) Pint of lager – half of which is sloshed on your Pete Doherty-signed t-shirt.

c) Pint of "red witch" of course – snakebite with Pernod and black.

d) Bottle of cheap merlot, guzzled in the toilets.

e) An exquisite cocktail of gin, lavender, lychee nectar and champagne, topped with an orchid garnish.

f) Strongbow, through a straw to avoid irritating your new tongue piercing.

g) A pint of that immense new Eastern European lager.

YOUR FAVOURITE PAIR OF SHOES ARE...

a) Dirtied, off-white, high-top Converse All Stars

b) Vintage leather brogues

c) Black leather, combat/5-inch platform boots

d) £3 plimsolls from Brick Lane, man

e) Red suede Chritian Louboutin maryjane wedges

f) Classic, checkerboard Van slip-ons

g) Literally, your new Velcro Lacoste trainers – sensible and stylish!

YOUR FAVOURITE PARTY SONG IS:

a) Love Will Tear Us Apart - Joy Division

b) Anything by Pete Doherty

c) Alice by Sisters of Mercy.
d) Standing in the Way of Control - The Gossip. As long as it's the Soulwax remix.
e) Walk this Way - Girls Aloud/Sugababes.
f) Dance Dance - Fall Out Boy.
g) Don't Look Back in Anger - Oasis. Nothing like an English classic.

WHICH BEST DESCRIBES YOUR TYPICAL NEW YEAR'S EVE?

a) Singing Auld Lang Syne, off key, arm in arm with your new best mate Nigel.
b) Sweating, jumping and swearing along to the Libertines' Fuck Forever.
c) Drinking blood red wine while your friend Siouxsie performs a ritual.
d) Dancing to hottest electro-grindie at a warehouse gathering in Shoreditch.
e) Snogging Danny Dyer in the bathroom at Studio Valbonne, oops!
f) Grounded in Stratford, waiting for your folks to fall asleep so you can sneak out.
g) Doing blow in the bathroom at your friend's private pub party in Essex.

THE RESULTS ARE IN:

Mostly As Drinking is a sport for you thus you belong at The Good Mixer where jaded Aussie bartenders blend nicely with the leathered clientele.

Mostly Bs Gig-going is your activity of choice, topped with a bit of Pete-stalking. Go to the Dublin Castle, where your idol is known to frequent.

Mostly Cs The Devonshire Arms bans sportswear and embraces the heavily eyelined - welcome home.

Mostly Ds Nothing like a Sunday piss-up with good chunes at the Lock Tavern. Get a roast and some fit bird's number.

Mostly Es Gutted when the Hawley burnt down, you are completely relieved that the exquisite Gilgamesh wasn't touched by the flames.

Mostly Fs You don't mind camping out at the train station as long as it means you make it on time for Underworld's daytime concert tomorrow - get in line.

Mostly Gs - If you must go to Camden, the Grand Union plays music at the right volume (not too loud), has sexy barmaids and they play the football too.

It's 2.30am You've just stumbled out of the Dublin Castle and no one is ready for the night to end. Camden Town is rammed with requisite crowds of crackheads, cybergoths and cider-intoxicated suburban teenagers spewing all sorts of profanities and puke from their make-up-smeared gobs. Steady yourselves and walk north, politely refusing the many offers of drugs (they'll be bad), hookers (they'll be worse) and minicabs (they'll be hookers) you'll encounter on the ten-minute stroll to Chalk Farm. After the market and Roundhouse, a little venue awaits your crew promising greasy food, cheap drinks and local music 'til the early hours.

Marathon Kebab opened in the late 1970s and began its operation as a late-night drinking spot 17 years ago when local musicians Bob and Dex played for the first time. Known lovingly as the Chippie Disco, Marathon was taken over in 2000 by the Boyraz family, and has become a favourite spot for late night boozing and live music. Enjoy jazz on Fridays and Saturdays, when musicians vie with punters for space in the tiny backroom bar. The rest of the week is known for its good ol' rock n' roll.

1

Marathon Kebab
87 Chalk Farm Rd
Chalk Farm
NW1 8AR
020 74853814
Beer: £2.80
Spirits: £3.00
Marathon Special
(rice, chips, kofte, chicken/lamb shish, dolmade) £6.50
Open until 4am

Watch the leaves flutter in the wind, angry in autumn, breezy in summer. Sue and Rodger Davis built their stunning Japanese-style home out of African teak, specially treated glass that traps in heat, and what looks to us like love. They made it in 1987, and share their peace-filled space with a handful of respectful guests. The house stands boldly on the corner of Camden Mews and Murray Street, and provides a welcome refuge from the flurry of Camden's streets. The only noise comes from Peckham, the 18-year-old Macaw. Lie back and enjoy.

Standard room: £50ppn (additional £5 fee for single-night stays) Spectacular corner double room: £60ppn A healthful breakfast of cereals, bread and fruit is included.

Japanese B&B
66 Camden Square
NW1 9XD
020 7485 4622

Stop talking. Rest your head. Be warm.

On the night of the 5th November 1605, Guido Fawkes and a band of fellow conspirators planned to assemble on a hilltop on Hampstead Heath to watch the Houses of Parliament blow up from a safe distance. But before they could strike a match and stand well back, the plot was rumbled, the explosion never happened and Guy, as his friends knew him, became one of the most famous martyrs in English history. **So it was that Parliament Hill got its name.** That's one story anyway. What's beyond doubt is that for hundreds of years Londoners have enjoyed that same awe-inspiring vantage point. Of course, in Guy's day Hampstead Heath was wild countryside, lying miles outside the city's boundaries. But with the advent of the railways, London's expansion exploded and the metropolis hungrily gobbled up Islington, Highgate and dozens of other satellite towns and villages and the fields surrounding them. The Heath could easily have suffered the same fate and been engulfed by row upon row of terraced housing. But thanks to some tireless campaigning by local do-gooders, the juggernaut of urbanisation was halted, leaving Hampstead Heath today as a wonderful anachronism, a bucolic island in the heart of the capital. It now serves both as London's Lungs, allowing the city to breathe, and as a playground for the population. Extensive recreational facilities mean there are at least 16 official sporting activities available, but it's the wilder parts of the Heath that make it a truly magical attraction. CS Lewis, HG Wells, Keats, Dickens, Coleridge, Orwell and Bill Oddie have all found inspiration here in this bewitching wonderland where surprises lurk around every corner. Ancient burial grounds, tumbledown cottages, strings of ponds, a grand stately home, the incredible old hamlet of Hatchett's Bottom (cunningly renamed the Vale of Health by Victorian estate agents), and 80s popstars shagging in the bushes are just some of the delights you might stumble across. Despite attracting some 10 million visitors a year, its 800 acres and wonderfully varied landscape – ponds, ravines, rolling meadows, enchanted forests – means it's quite easy to lose yourself completely and leave London and the 21st century behind.

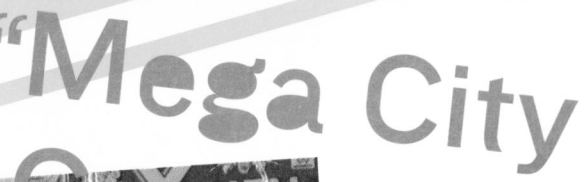

"Mega City Comics. Collecting past futures since 1986."

Inverness Street Market
18 Inverness Street,
NW1 7HJ,
020 7485 9320

Tube Mice

Sit on the furthest bench on the westbound
Central Line platform at Liverpool Street.
Keep quiet. Wait.
Watch the brickwork to your right – little sooty faces will appear.
Some call them pests but they're among my favourite Londoners.
Quiet (they understand you don't ever bother people on the Tube),
green (recycling all that fast food – boxes and all) and nocturnal
(sometimes it's good to not be the only creature on the platform).

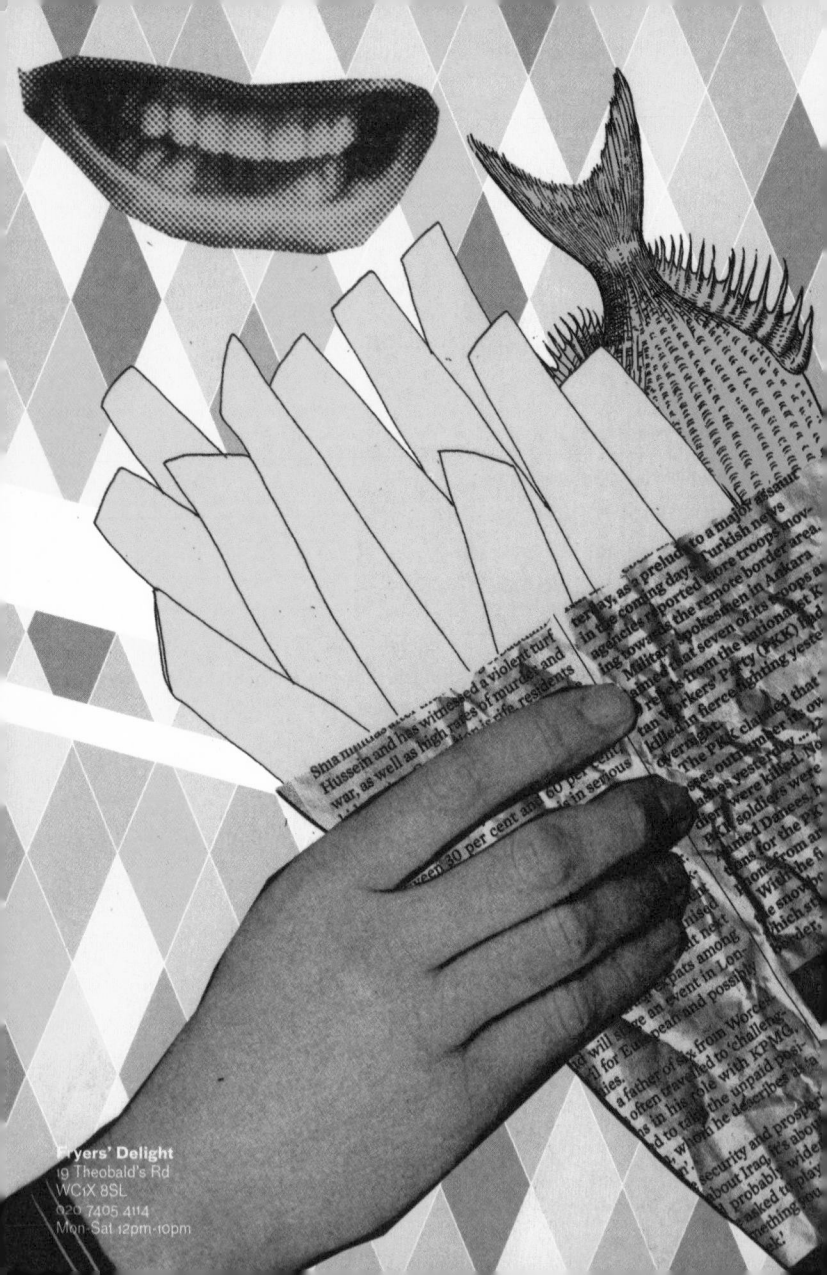

Scott's is the kind of place that filmmakers use as shorthand for London. Elegant and slightly staid, champagne and oysters, a smattering of celebs, with waiters so smooth they could be on castors.

Oysters are fine, but there's a different fish restaurant that people cross London for. The Fryers' Delight has everything you ask for in a proper chippy: formica tables, bread and butter with your supper, and you can bring your own booze. Your choice.

Fish vs Chips

Scott's
20 Mount Street
W1
020 7495 7309
Mon-Sun 12pm-3.30pm, 5.30pm-12am

Dealers vs Dogs

Aspinall's
28 Curzon Street,
020 7499 4599

Well, the dogs is cheaper. You can pay your entrance, have a bet or two and drown your sorrows in a beer and a hotdog for less than the price of a martini in <u>Aspinall's</u>.

Still, it's hard to live out your James Bond fantasies on <u>Plough Lane...</u>

GRA Wimbledon Stadium
Plough Lane
SW17 0BL
0870 840 8905
Tuesdays, Fridays and Saturdays
6.30pm-10.30pm

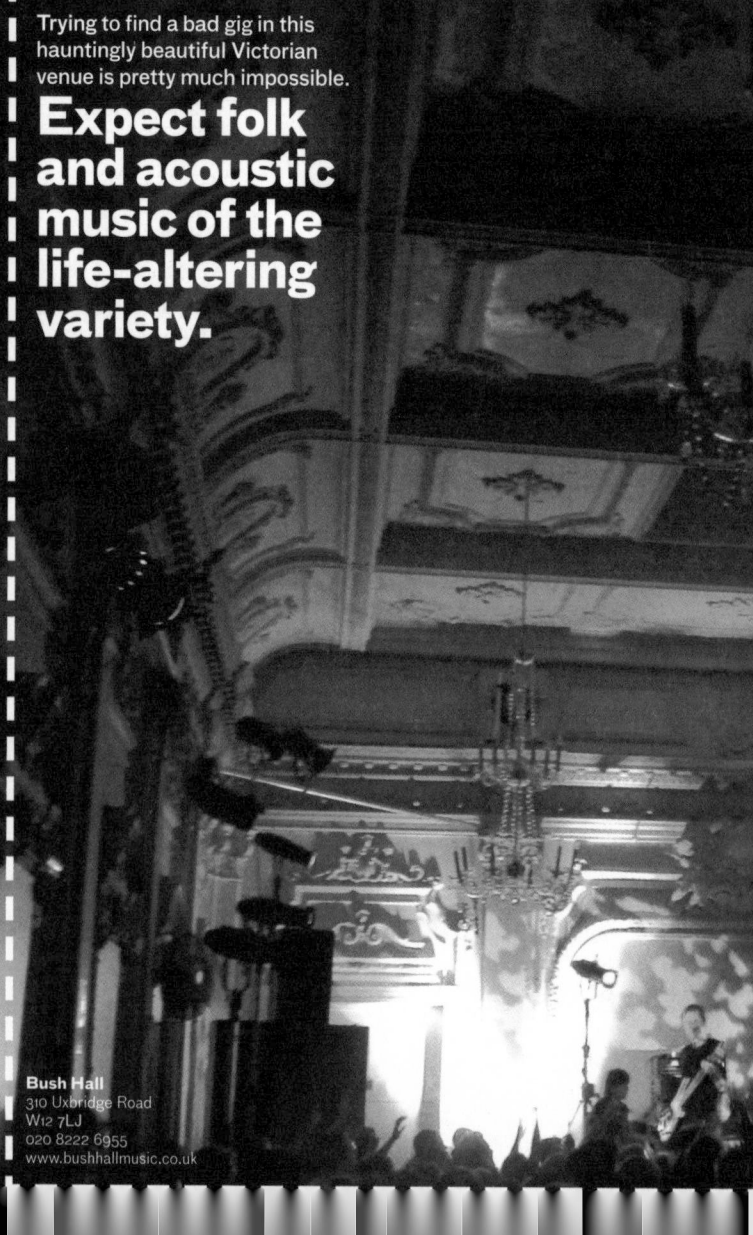

Trying to find a bad gig in this hauntingly beautiful Victorian venue is pretty much impossible.

Expect folk and acoustic music of the life-altering variety.

Bush Hall
310 Uxbridge Road
W12 7LJ
020 8222 6955
www.bushhallmusic.co.uk

Outside, you're sure you're in the wrong place.

A block of ex-council flats like any other, the tiny, fifth-floor window decorated with floral curtains. Then you step inside and there it is. A 40-foot airplane wing built straight through the house. To get to the bath or to make a cup of green tea, artist Steven Tyscko has to scurry under the huge curve of the wing, making a large statement about 9/11 and perhaps a bigger one about the commitment of artists 'living with their work'. The whole thing's for sale – flat, wing and all – but before it goes you can still go visit. Details at www.phlight.org

More than 20,000 forty-fives in blank cardboard sleeves line the back room of Ray and Steve's Jukebox Showroom. If you buy one of their vintage jukeboxes, you can fill it with whatever you like – for £3.50 a pop, they'll even get your favourite tune transferred to vinyl for you. Pop by, get Steve to make you a cup of tea - he makes a great cup of tea - and punch up *Suspicious Minds* on the Seeburg 200. Three minutes and twenty-eight seconds later, you're ready to throw your iPod away.

The Jukebox Showroom
9 Park Parade
Gunnersbury Avenue
W3 9BD
020 8992 8482/3
www.jukeboxshowroom.co.uk
Mon- Sat, 10:30am-5pm

It's a
strange
beast, the
Frontline.

Set up by a group of British independent newsmen over a boozy Christmas dinner during the Romanian revolution, it's part war-correspondents' club, part restaurant and part private museum. The ground floor's a fantastic airy dining room serving glammed-up versions of classic British food, and some great wines. (The list is by wine writer Malcolm Gluck, and instead of the usual percentage mark-up, the club always adds just a tenner plus VAT, so if you're buying a more expensive bottle there are some serious bargains to be had.) Upstairs is a kind of world-affairs forum. Guest speakers, usually journalists with hands-on experience of the world's trouble spots, give weekly talks that delve into the real stories behind the spin. And in between the two is the members' club. You'll have to sweet-talk a member to get in, but they're a friendly bunch, especially if you're buying. Inside is all manner of war memorabilia – Andy McNabb's escape plans, a mobile phone shattered by a sniper's bullet (and so saving a man's life), and strange kitschery like lanyards courtesy of Hezbollah. They also do a mean martini.

The Frontline
13 Norfolk Place
W2 1QJ
020 7479 8960
Mon-Sat 10am-10.30pm;
Sun 10am-4pm
www.frontlineclub.com

Don't expect to be in and out in ten minutes, this little deli does serious sandwiches and they w● be rushed. You can go buy the paper, sit yourself down and be● halfway through the sport page● by the time your food comes, b● it's well worth the wait – try the omelette and avocado sandwic● and you won't be complaining.

Minkies
3 Unicorn House
Station Terrace
NW10 5RS
020 8969 2182

Mornings in Kensal Rise are all about Minkies...

...and evenings are all about Samson Miro

Samson Miro
75 Chamberlayne R●
NW10 3ND
020 8962 0275

From the moment this little wine shop put in one long wooden table the place has been packed. Why? Cos the wine's good, the people are passionate and they never talk down to you. Last night a guy came in with a takeaway pizza and asked for something to go with it. In lots of shops he'd have been met with disdain but not here. The question was simply, "Interesting.. what toppings?"

Classic boozing. Real ale. Two words that have an uncanny ability to strike fear into the heart of the uninitiated lager drinkers among us. However, here we have a drink with infinite permutations, lovingly crafted by brewers up and down the country. Here is your chance to see one of the biggest breweries in London, to be educated in the complicated process from the grain storage to the fermentation, and to learn the history of both the building and the company behind it. Yes there is a tasting, and yes the more you hang around and ask questions, the more likely you are to be offered a taste of one of the limited edition Vintage bottles they have hanging around the back of the bar. After starting the day at the brewery it would make sense to continue drinking down by the river... Stroll along the river taking note of the floodlines and the expensive houses and soon you will find The Dove, tucked away down a small passage on the riverfront. Dating back to the 17th century, it's a cosy and popular spot to drink Fuller's ales and spend a summer's afternoon overlooking the Thames, or a winters evening warming the cockles by the open fire. It has the smallest bar in Britain – but you won't have to wait long to get served, so settle down and enjoy a traditional setting that in the past has entranced the likes of Graham Greene and Ernest Hemingway. Next you will come to the Black Lion, a good spot for lunch with a gastro menu and pleasant atmosphere. It's bigger than it looks from the outside and with board games available as well, it would be easy to spend the rest of the afternoon in here. It is more than 200 years old, and was originally opened by a pig farmer whose homebrew took off so well he changed career. Local author A.P. Herbert wrote about the pub under the name 'Black Swan' in The Water Gypsies. Along the stretch to Hammersmith Bridge there are numerous places to stop for refreshment. In the summer, crowds at The Old Ship burst out onto the lawn while its many dining rooms are always rammed. If the crowds are too much for you, try a little further down, where The Blue Anchor, an 18th-century drinking den in which the composer Holst supposedly wrote *Hammersmith*, has tables by the river overlooking the bridge. I was drawn in by the lights. Neon beer signs don't usually work but here they add to the feel of being in some central European drinking den. It's tiny inside, but you'll always feel welcome, and the size doesn't stop them putting on live music – which may be a good thing, if you don't want to talk to your friends anyway...

Blue Anchor   The Black Lion   Fullers Brewery Tour

Pickwick's Wine Bar   The Dove

Blue Anchor
13 Lower Mall
W6 9DJ
020 8748 5774

The Black Lion
South Black Lion
Lane
W6 9TJ
020 8748 2639

Pickwick's Wine Bar
13 Devonshire Road
W4 2EU
020 8747 1824

Fullers
Chiswick Lane
South
W4 2QB
020 8996 2000

The Dove
19 Upper Mall
W6 9TA
020 8748 5405

It's 4.30 am. You're in the back of a cab and you're hungry. Not quick-get-me-a-kebab-to-soak-up-the-booze hungry, but hungry hungry. Your choices? Fried chicken, bagels or Vingt Quatre. Love the eggs Benedict, the blantant checking out and the tables of Chelsea types with a few drinks inside them and lowered expectations since they didn't manage to pull Prince Harry/Kylie. Don't love the queues, but hey where else are you getting gnocchi and Pinot Grigio as the sun comes up?

Vingt Quatre
325 Fulham Road
SW10 9QL
020 7376 7224

Down the concrete stairwells of the South Bank they come. Vaulting off the handrails, sneakers scuffing the walls, hitting the ground rolling and away in a burst of laughter...

...but if you want to join them in a bit of free-running, how d'you learn? Well there's just one place. Started by parkour legend EZ, the classes at the <u>Moberly</u> are a blast. Beginning with odd rolls and crawls, working up to explosive leaps and somersaults, a mixed bag of free-runners aged between 10 to 50, are getting ready to take to the streets.

Moberly Sports Centre
Kilburn Lane
W10 4AH
Fridays 7.30pm-9.30pm

Reachable only by footbridge, Eel Pie Island rises out of the water like a sleepy behemoth. Boathouses and homes with picket-fenced gardens sit where once stood the Eel Pie Hotel – a centre for London's counterculture in the 1950s and 1960s. The hotel is no more but artists still channel the spirit of the island to this day. **Eel Pie Island got its name when Henry VIII began to stop by to feast on the island's speciality.** Merrymakers were noted on the island as early as 1750 – for Londoners who couldn't afford the seaside, this was the place to go. In 1830, the Eel Pie Hotel opened, hosting tea dances on its sprung dance floor. Dickens came to the party, and the island is mentioned in Nicholas Nickelby: "Unto the Eel Pie Island at Twickenham... to dance in the open air to the music of a locomotive band." In the 1950s, the hotel's status as a bohemian playground was secured with its trad jazz night, where musicians such as George Melly and Acker Bilk played. Melly described the run-down hotel, with its ornate columns and arches, as like "something from a Tennessee Williams novel". In the 1960s, local boy Mick Jagger played in an R&B band on the pub circuit, and the Eel Pie Club at the hotel embraced the burgeoning scene. It was soon a place that parents feared, due to the influx of young people looking to procure booze, drugs and wanton sex. **Musicians who played included The Stones, Rod Stewart, David Jones (later Bowie), The Who and the Yardbirds.** Kids came and danced, then during the interval would step out onto the riverbank for a sneaky spliff. In 1967, the hotel closed due to a massive repair bill but reopened briefly in 1971 as a rock haven, featuring Black Sabbath, Pink Floyd and Led Zeppelin. Then, after an order for demolition, the hotel burnt down in a 'mysterious' fire. Thirty-odd years on, the island has 120 inhabitants in 40 homes and, like any community where people try to escape the norm, there's a mood of open-mindedness coupled with a sense of seclusion. The artistic tradition lives on in those songwriters who still inhabit the island, led by the father-and-son proponents of Thamesbeat, the Mystery Jets. "It's in London, but not in London. Whenever you come here it feels like the weekend," says Mystery Jet dad Henry Harrison. In the early noughties, the Jets threw legendary parties on the island where musicians such as Larrikin Love, Jamie T and the Noisettes would play in between stand-up comics, poets and random orators. It was an eclectic mix in keeping with the island's bohemian spirit and utopian leanings.

Take a train to Twickenham, go down to the river's edge and gaze out over the Thames

QUIET.

IF YOU'RE TALKING
WHEN A BAND IS
PLAYING
WE'LL TELL YOU TO
SHUT UP.

Back in the day the only musical fun to be had on the <u>**Kilburn High Road**</u> **were covers from the bands set up in the corner of every Irish pub (***Smells Like Teen Spirit*** with a penny whistle and a fiddle – I was there). But three new venues are turning this stretch of Little Dublin into the new Camden...**

We could talk about all the bands who played their breakthrough gig there. Or tell you how they helped make the Kilburn High Road hip again. We could tell you tales of sweaty club nights and riotous concerts. But we can't say a word. The band's on.

The Luminaire
311 High Road
NW6 7JR

Locals didn't know what hit them. Ed from the Chemical Brothers DJing in what was once Kilburn's dodgiest pub? (And that's a title with some competition.) Dim sum in the week and roasts at the weekend? Sleek new pool tables without a rip or a missing ball? Even, whisper it, cocktails?

The Westbury
34 Kilburn High Road
NW6 5UA

An excellent free jukebox, odd little film and comedy nights and the hippest new bands make the Good Ship our favourite late-night Kilburn venue.

The Good Ship
289 Kilburn High Road
NW6 7JR
07949 008253
Mon-Thurs till 2am
Fri-Sat till 4am. Sun till 2am

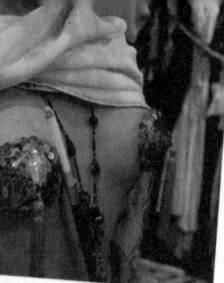

The Girl Can't Help It
Any stall owned by people called Sparkle Moore and Cad van Swankster has got to be good. Spectacular 1950s clothes and knick-knacks ranging from sequinned plushies for all your burlesque needs, to a dress once worn by Marilyn Monroe.

Tony Durante
A tiny stall dripping with uber-bling costume jewellery, huge Jackie-O sunglasses and jazz-era vintage handbags.

There's nothing stuffy about Alfie's Market

At heart it's closer to the organised chaos of the scruffy street market outside than to the classic antiques shops that line Church Street. This isn't a gallery – the stall-holders gossip and haggle, and the best things on sale are meant to be used, not looked at. You could easily spend a day here – there's a cosy little café at the back – but here are some highlights.

Dodo Posters
Classic Art Deco and modernist graphic design stall covered from floor to ceiling in posters, adverts and packaging.

Alfie's Market
13-25 Chruch Street,
NW8 8DT,
0207 723 6066

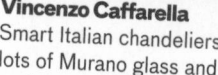

Vincenzo Caffarella
Smart Italian chandeliers, lots of Murano glass and sculptural-looking lamps.

Whatever it is, it's three or four blissful hours when the world of work just doesn't exist.

There are few deeper pleasures in life than taking a sickie from work, loading up on sugar-based snack products and catching a double bill at the Riverside. Sometimes it's arty – Cassavetes or an Alejandro Gonzales Inarritu season. Sometimes it's trashy – road movies or old musicals back-to-back, and you just slide further down your seat and bask in it.

Riverside Studios
Crisp Road
W6 9RL
020 8237 1111
www.riversidestudios.co.uk

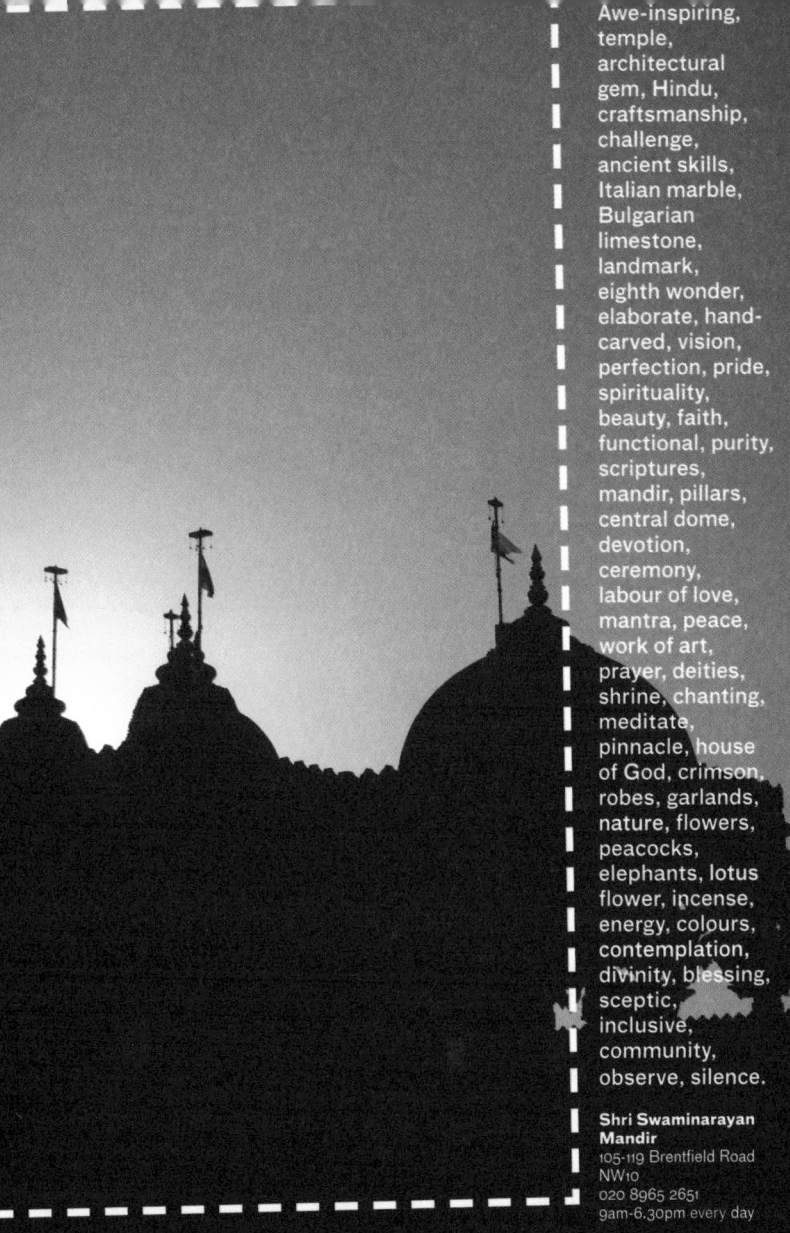

Awe-inspiring, temple, architectural gem, Hindu, craftsmanship, challenge, ancient skills, Italian marble, Bulgarian limestone, landmark, eighth wonder, elaborate, hand-carved, vision, perfection, pride, spirituality, beauty, faith, functional, purity, scriptures, mandir, pillars, central dome, devotion, ceremony, labour of love, mantra, peace, work of art, prayer, deities, shrine, chanting, meditate, pinnacle, house of God, crimson, robes, garlands, nature, flowers, peacocks, elephants, lotus flower, incense, energy, colours, contemplation, divinity, blessing, sceptic, inclusive, community, observe, silence.

Shri Swaminarayan Mandir
105-119 Brentfield Road
NW10
020 8965 2651
9am-6.30pm every day

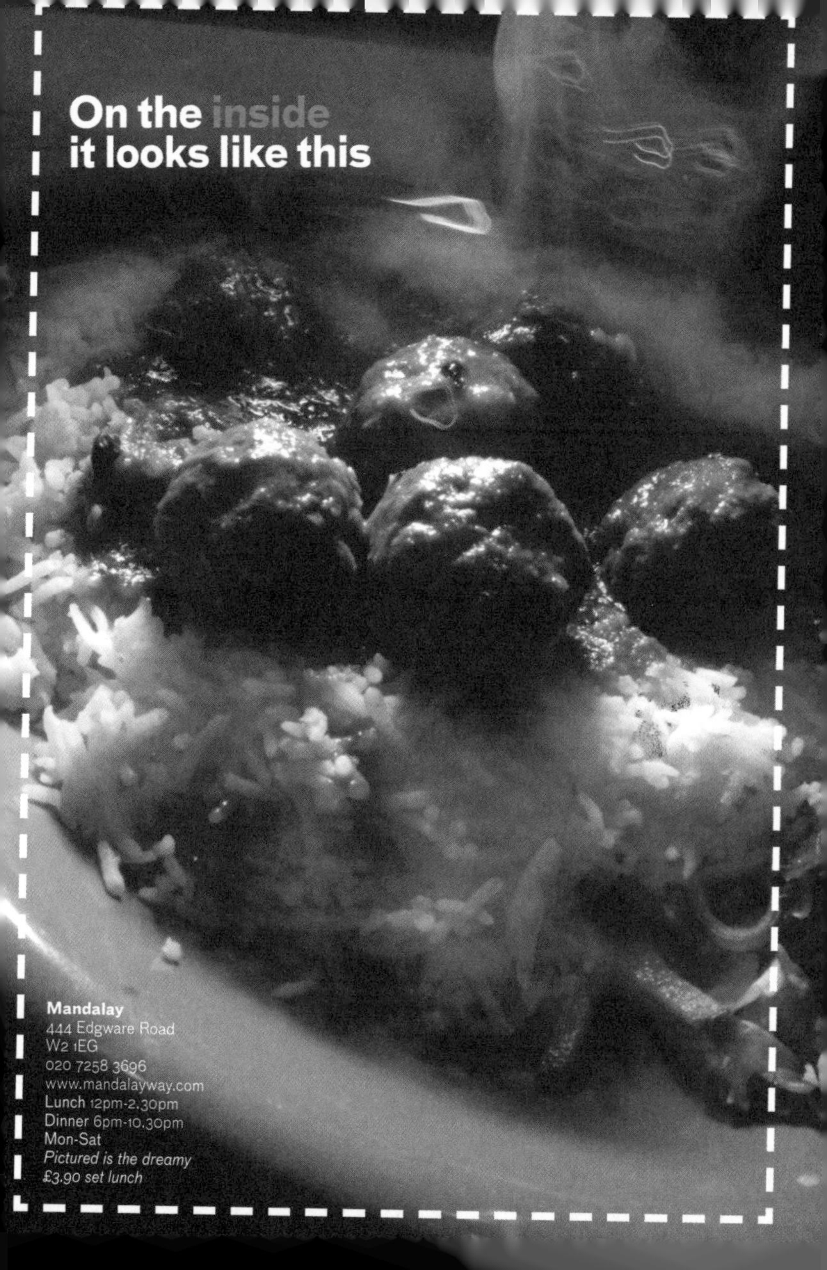

On the inside
it looks like this

Mandalay
444 Edgware Road
W2 1EG
020 7258 3696
www.mandalayway.com
Lunch 12pm-2.30pm
Dinner 6pm-10.30pm
Mon-Sat
*Pictured is the dreamy
£3.90 set lunch*

They really shouldn't work well together – Latin America's sunny grooves and laid-back lives transplanted to grey old London – but luckily for us Brazilians, Columbians, Mexicans and the rest all seem to love this city They get concrete and clay and general decay, and we get...

Coma y Punto

94-95 Granville Arcade
Coldharbour Lane
Brixton
SW9 8PS
020 7326 0276
Take cash – although this joint loves plastic, it won't take it as payment.
Mesmerisingly Colombian, right down to the bottled soft drinks. It's a little anomaly on the fringe of Granville Arcade, but it has a big Latin American following, so get there early for Saturday lunch or you'll miss out on some big hunks of meat, Bogotá-style.

Barrio North

45 Essex Rd
Islington
N1 2SF
With Mexican wrestling masks on the wall, American comic-book pages in the toilet cubicles, multicoloured mosaic tiling zagging and zigging around you, it's a warm and friendly pan-Latin American mashup. Clink your Quilmes in a glowing caravan of love to some choice music down the Barrio.

The Barraco Café

10 Kingsgate Place
Kilburn
NW6 4TA
020 7604 4664
Reinaldo Morato has the best Brazilian boteco in London. It says so on his business card. And it's probably true. Inside you'll find that world-famous Brazilian warmth in the feijoada stew, the service, and the music DVDs that glow on a TV behind the counter. Barraco is tucked away off Kilburn High Road, unpolluted by stragglers but easily get-to-able. Try to the açaí with granola, banana and honey and hang out for a long, long time – that's how Brazilians do it best.

Guanabara

Parker St
WC2B 5PW
020 7242 8600
If you love being surrounded by pissed City types ogling foreign girls, come to Guanabara between 5pm and 7.30pm on a weeknight ("happy hour"). OK, don't come to Guanabara at happy hour. Any other time of the week, and especially at weekends, this place is an absolute delight, photogenic Latin American London on an epic scale. Worth hanging on for a great end-of-the-night party spirit.

Favela Chic

91- 93 Great Eastern St
EC2A
020 7613 5228
Those São Paulo hip cats at Jungle Drums magazine say this is where the knife-edge cool latinos and latinas go to shake it. Despite its ghetto name, Favela Chic is rather boutique-y – its first branch opened in Paris – and also appears to have a refreshingly small wankers-to-square-metre ratio for the Shoreditch-Hoxton-Old Street zooniverse.

Batmacumba

www.batmacumba.com
DJ Cliffy takes his show around town – you can often catch him at the ICA, if he's not working on projects out in Recife. He's a DJ with a lot of soul and bags of uplifting records, and a Cliffy gig is a proper multimedia event with its heart in all the right places. Dance all night without a pout in sight.

London is the best place to get a Ruby Murray outside the **Indian subcontinent**, curry here is as ubiquitous as fish 'n' chips due to the diaspora of folk who've moved to the smoke from Kathmandu to Colombo. However, on every street corner lurks a curry house under the misapprehension that their food is edible, so chose your eatery wisely. Here's our trusty guide to the curry capital.

Punjab

Sitara
784 Holloway Road
Archway N19
020 7281 0649

I've got a sneaking feeling that Raj Parikh is the only restaurateur fusing curry and jazz in London today, and this venture has won several awards. The deep red walls with photos of jazz artists, and great music make this the most atmospheric of places to get a pakora. The service can be slow but when your food arrives you won't care – the prawn bhuna is the talk of the town.

Kerala

Radha Krishna Bhavan
86 Tooting High Street
SW17
020 8682 0969

Radha and Krisha are the Romeo and Juliet of Hinduism, so the décor is full-on romantic-kitsch, with giant sunset and palm tree friezes on the wall. This place is stamped with the Keralan seal, and a colourfully costumed statue of a kathakali dancer observes from the corner. To sample food from the spice capital of India, try cashew nut pakoda, the traditionally spiced seafood dishes, uthappam, dry stir-fried vegetables (thoran) or black chickpea curry (kadala).

North India

Safa
22 Camberwell Church St
SE5
020 7252 4800

The jewel in Camberwell's culinary crown is this sleek, modern curry house representing Delhi and Mumbai. I always start with the crispest spicy poppadoms and mint sauce, then I have to order the exquisite chickpea curry seasoned with red onions and the tender paneer chilli masala. The chef's speciality, tiger prawn balchou, boasts succulent prawns in a fragrant masala sauce.

Bangladesh

Preem
118-122 Brick Lane
E1 6RL
020 7247 0397

Murad rocks – he's the genial host with the crazy Hoxton-style mullet at the best balti house in Banglatown. I would give most restaurants on Brick Lane a miss as the food is bland and swills in oil but Preem is different. I recommend the chicken madras, which is subtly seasoned, or the roast leg of lamb – sizzling-hot when brought to the table. You'll soon see why Preem stands out among the rest.

Sri Lanka

The Sekara
3 Lower Grosvenor Place
SW1W 0EJ
020 7834 0722

I'm Sri Lankan, and a fussy foodie, so this place has a lot to live up to but totally delivers. The menu is cheap as chips but the décor isn't drab and regulars come in droves. Nibble on fish patties, mutton rolls and vadai, just like my aunty makes. What's great is that the chef goes home regularly to stock up on authentic spices so even the dhal here is different, flavoured with lemongrass. For traditional home-style dishes, sample string hoppers or kothu roti – shredded and stir-fried with a choice of meat or veg. To cool down get sweet on wattalapam, a dessert with coconut milk, juggery,

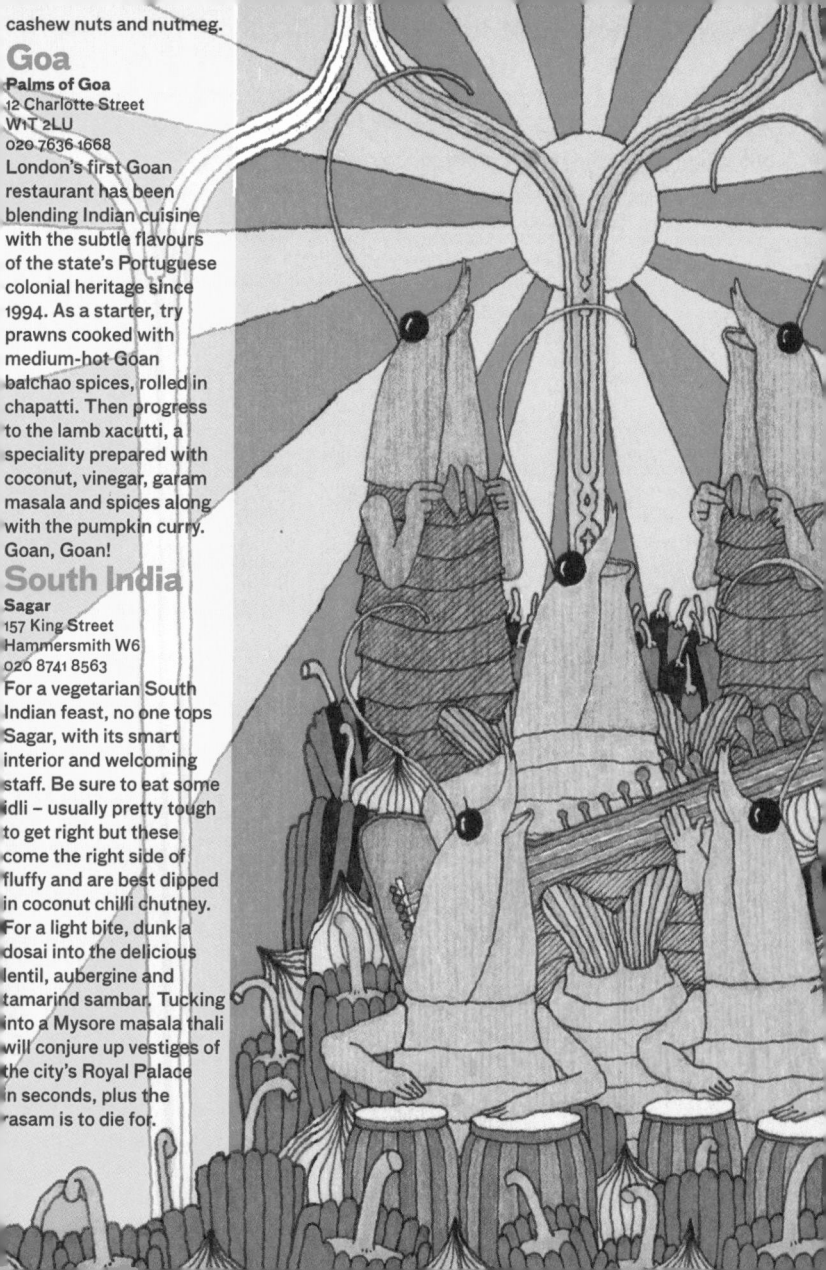

cashew nuts and nutmeg.

Goa

Palms of Goa
12 Charlotte Street
W1T 2LU
020 7636 1668

London's first Goan restaurant has been blending Indian cuisine with the subtle flavours of the state's Portuguese colonial heritage since 1994. As a starter, try prawns cooked with medium-hot Goan balchao spices, rolled in chapatti. Then progress to the lamb xacutti, a speciality prepared with coconut, vinegar, garam masala and spices along with the pumpkin curry. Goan, Goan!

South India

Sagar
157 King Street
Hammersmith W6
020 8741 8563

For a vegetarian South Indian feast, no one tops Sagar, with its smart interior and welcoming staff. Be sure to eat some idli – usually pretty tough to get right but these come the right side of fluffy and are best dipped in coconut chilli chutney. For a light bite, dunk a dosai into the delicious lentil, aubergine and tamarind sambar. Tucking into a Mysore masala thali will conjure up vestiges of the city's Royal Palace in seconds, plus the rasam is to die for.

Did you know that an estimated 7% of Londoners are of Jamaican descent? That is probably why Caribbean food is rarely done badly in this crazy ole town. Across the pretty city you'll find plenty of spots serving peppery jerk chicken, home-baked beef patties and scrumptious goat curry. Pass one of these by and you'll kick yourself later.

East

Peppers and Spice
Kingsland Road
E8 2JP

Outstanding takeaway serving jerk, curry goat (which you can cut with a sponge), stewed mutton, and homemade patties. Has a queue out the door all day, every day. Puts everywhere else in the shade.

West

Yum Yum Caribbean Takeaway
312 Ladbroke Grove
W10 5NQ
020 8968 1477

Best known for its variety of patties, Yum Yum also serves the usual range of curries, goat, oxtail, jerk, fish and a house specialty fried chicken. Comes highly recommended by le cool readers.

Central

Jerk City
89 Wardour Street
W1F 8ZD
020 7287 2878

A popular spot with central London workers, this Soho eatery can get packed at lunchtime, so prepare to wait. Try the ackee and saltfish. Takeaway available too.

South

Negril
132 Brixton Hill
SW2 1RS
020 8674 8798

You're spoilt for choice for great Caribbean food in this part of town but Nigril's a cut above the rest. On a sunny morning you can see streams of locals traipsing up Brixton Hill, following their noses

Bisto Kids-style to where the jerk chicken is being cooked outside on giant oil drums. You've got to try the Blue Mountain coffee.

North

Kyla's Kitchen
149 York Way
N7 9LG

Tucked up on York Way in the no-man's land between Camden Town, Holloway Road and King's Cross, Kyla's is a quirky gem among the scruff. For five quid you get a massive helping of rice and peas, jerk chicken (or stew, or oxtail or goat) and homemade coleslaw on the side.

Café 202 for
your breakfast.

To your left the
swish Rodeo-Drive-
in-the rain of
Westbourne Grove.

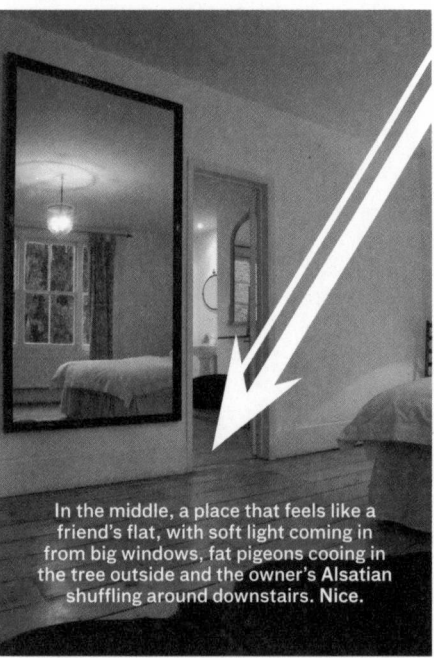

To your right
scruffy old
Portobello.

In the middle, a place that feels like a
friend's flat, with soft light coming in
from big windows, fat pigeons cooing in
the tree outside and the owner's **Alsatian**
shuffling around downstairs. **Nice.**

The Lonsdale for cocktails.
The Tiroler Hut for late nights.

Main House
6 Colville Road
W11 2BP
020 7221 9691

An Iraqi souvenir stand.

A recreation of a mews street with every stall housing a different variety of fortune-teller

20 or 30 miniscule computer shops flogging everything from circuit boards to blank CDs with everything about half the price of Dixons up the road.

Lots of manicurists

lestinian café.

It looks like any one of the thousands of little tourist-tat-and-cheap-rucksack shops that line Queensway. But step through number 23 and you'll find a huge warren of tiny stalls, including:

A Thai café.

A shop selling thousands of 50p Russian VHSs.

The world's saddest lonely heart's board. Seriously, don't read this if you're an emotional type.

A dodgy Brazilian bikini shop.

And, best of all, Samovar – a tiny, four-table Russian restaurant packed with people who work at the nearby embassy. It's authentic as they come – you might have to ask for an English menu – and heartily cheap. Have the dumplings. That's less a recommendation than a necessity because the menu's very dumpling heavy. And have the kimmel. That *is* a recommendation. How often do you get to find out what strawberry-flavoured Milk of Magnesia would taste like?

Queensway Arcade
23 Queensway
Bayswater
W2 4QP

There's a certain moment, after a few rounds of beers in frosted steins and chilled Jagermeister shots...

...when the birthday girl has finished playing Edelweiss on the bells and is tucking into her fondue...

...and everyone's dancing to owner Jo in his lederhosen, playing the saxophone...

...and old German guys are singing "Ein Prosit" in the corner...

...when this is the greatest bar in the city...

Tiroler Hut
27 Westbourne Grove
W2 4UA
020 7727 3981
Tues-Sat 6.30pm-1am, Sun 6.30pm-11pm

Stylists are browsing the racks, pulling out pieces for some video. There's cursing from the cave-like basement where new purchases are getting ironed. Owners Fiona and Claire are altering stuff and trying to sort out their weekends on the phone. There's a kind of organised chaos at Rellik that'd make the place appealing even if they didn't have the best stock of vintage gear in the capital. But they do and it's that gear that pulls people in. The Japanese make a pilgrimage for the Vivienne Westwood, Italians pick up classic Prada and Pucci, and the New Rave kids save up for the plastic jewellery and day-glo eightieswear.

"You know that feeling in a secondhand shop when you've been looking through suits that people died in and acrylic shirts and shoes with only one heel and then you find just the greatest, most beautiful thing and your heart stops because it's just so perfect? Rellik's like that. But all the time. With every single item."

Rellik
At the foot of Trellick Tower
8 Golborne Road
W10 5NW
020 8962 0089

If you're in Rellik then you're just seconds from some of London's best soup. Head back down the Golborne Road. Keep to the right. Don't get distracted by the Lisboa Patisserie – you can get coffee there afterwards. See the white van on the roadside, with a bunch of Moroccan guys next to it eating chips in a bap? Pull up a stool, order the soup – the chickpea's the best – and a Coke in a glass bottle. Enjoy, and enjoy also getting change from three quid.

Golborne Road
W10

If it's raining, try <u>Maramia</u>. London's first Palestinian café is a laidback joy – the owner's son crawls through in his nappy, there's a constant stream of people popping in for a sage tea and a chat, and the food is goooooooooooooooooooooooooooood.

Maramia
48 Golborne Road
W10 5PR
020 3132 3431
www.maramia.com

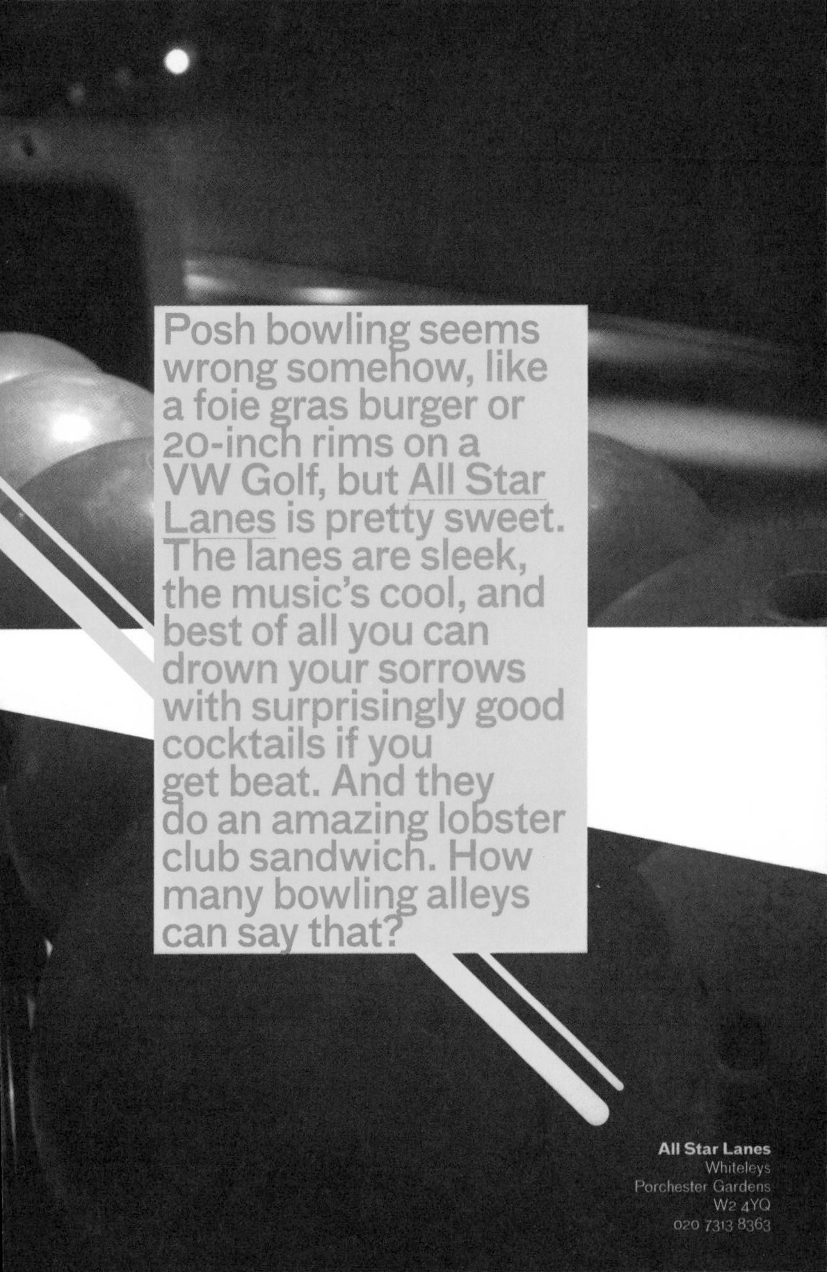

Posh bowling seems wrong somehow, like a foie gras burger or 20-inch rims on a VW Golf, but All Star Lanes is pretty sweet. The lanes are sleek, the music's cool, and best of all you can drown your sorrows with surprisingly good cocktails if you get beat. And they do an amazing lobster club sandwich. How many bowling alleys can say that?

All Star Lanes
Whiteleys
Porchester Gardens
W2 4YQ
020 7313 8363

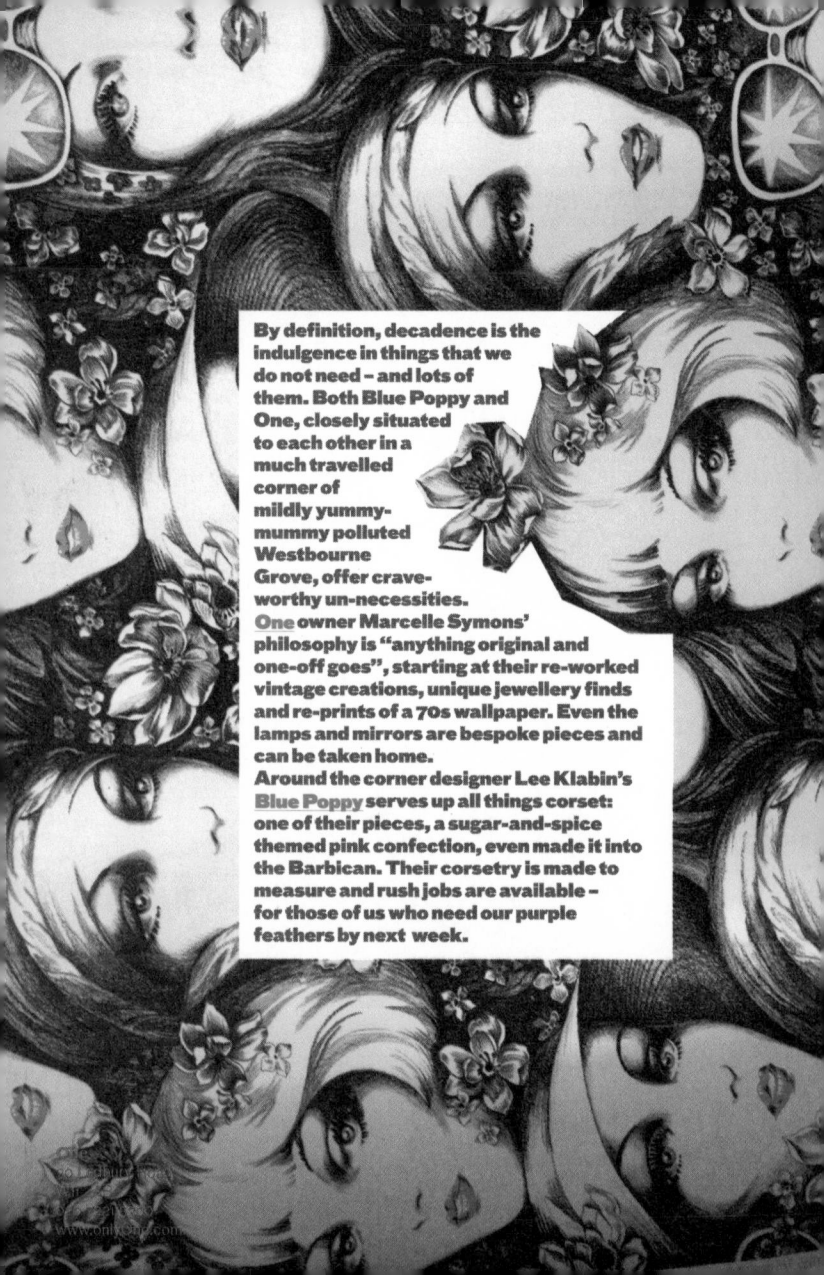

By definition, decadence is the indulgence in things that we do not need – and lots of them. Both Blue Poppy and One, closely situated to each other in a much travelled corner of mildly yummy-mummy polluted Westbourne Grove, offer crave-worthy un-necessities.

One owner Marcelle Symons' philosophy is "anything original and one-off goes", starting at their re-worked vintage creations, unique jewellery finds and re-prints of a 70s wallpaper. Even the lamps and mirrors are bespoke pieces and can be taken home.

Around the corner designer Lee Klabin's **Blue Poppy** serves up all things corset: one of their pieces, a sugar-and-spice themed pink confection, even made it into the Barbican. Their corsetry is made to measure and rush jobs are available – for those of us who need our purple feathers by next week.

Blue Poppy
171 Westbourne Grove
W11 2RS
020 77929667
www.bluepoppycouture.com

Drinks served in flaming volcanoes, huge murals of that green-skinned Chinese lady, a monthly rum club and kitschy music. The only serious thing about Trailer Happiness is the cocktail list.

Trailer Happiness
177 Portobello Road
W11 2DY
0207 727 2700

Attracted by the prospect of reassuringly expensive restaurants and hot-and-cold running Hugh Grants, American bankers and movie moguls have turned Westbourne Grove into a kind of mini USA. The prime spot to watch this well-heeled and well-groomed tribe walk by is from the corner table outside Café 202. Newcomers may prefer the quiet back garden (walk all the way through the Nicole Fahri shop), but we like to watch the beautiful people from out front. The Yanks love 202's bacon and real maple syrup; we prefer the unsurpassable scrambled eggs and mushrooms.

Café 202
Nicole Fahri
202 Westbourne Grove
W11 2RH
020 7792 6888

You catch little glimpses of it from Westbourne Grove. There's a classical bust in a high window, velvet curtains lit by grand chandeliers... but nothing really prepares you for the first time you step into <u>Miller's</u>. Every wall, every table, every surface is encrusted with antiques. Classical statues hide Art Deco posters and kitsch Victorian figurines. A battered baby grand props up a human skull, a horseback Trojan and silver candelabra. And the whole place is the setting for a kind of 21st-century Grand Salon. Writers, artists and thinkers come from all over the world to speak here. If you come to witness a thoughtful piece of oratory, always plan to stay for drinks afterwards – it's included in the price, and that's when the real discussions take place.

Miller's Academy
of Arts and Sciences
28a Hereford Road
W2 5AJ
020 7229 5103
www.rooms-hire-locations-
lectures-debates.co.uk

Each

step

down

the

dark

corridors

of

Miller's

Hotel

takes you further from this world and this time

Miller's Hotel
111a Westbourne Grove
W2 4UW
020 7243 1024
www.millersuk.com

Just one look at the queues of tourists, Notting Hill locals and out-of-town sugar junkies tells you what need to know: the Hummingbird Bakery makes the best damn cupcakes in the city.

Hummingbird Bakery
133 Portobello Road
W11 2DY
020 7229 6446
www.hummingbirdbakery.com
Tues-Sat 10am-5.30pm, Sun 11am-5pm

When you have a cocktail made for you exactly how it's supposed to be made, using techniques and recipes perfected over hundreds of years, then you'll never go to a chain bar again. At the Lonsdale, top mixologists Henry Besant and Dick Bradsell have created a London-specific menu – all the rums originate from ex-British colonies, for example (apart from Cuba) - and trace the signature drinks of ages past in the city. And for a very well-to-do place in Notting Hill, the prices are remarkably low for what are some of the very best-mixed drinks in the country.

Lonsdale
48 Lonsdale Road
W11 2DE

Some might say that cycling London's roads is adventure enough.

Cycle paths are scant, drivers are irritable and the roads run from the hilly to the badly repaired. This constant background hum of danger gives an adrenalin boost that if administered in any other form would be illegal, so eyes, ears, nose, pedals and wits must be kept at their sharpest. If you want to keep that rush going after your commute home, London has a few cycling surprises in store.

Alleycats
Of dubious legality, questionable safety but heart-pounding excitement, these roughly organised street races are a recent import from New York. You won't see them advertised anywhere, but hang around cycle courier spots – Velorution on Great Titchfield Street or www.movingtargetzine.

com – and they'll come to light. Warning: these are fiendishly complex routes through backstreets, pavements and car parks, and competitors are seriously fit individuals – no Sunday cyclists or bomb-dodgers here. Their penchant for themed races (Star Wars characters, pirates) mean you might suffers the indignity of being soundly thrashed by a girl in a Wookie costume.

Roller Racing
Back in the 50s Roller Racing – a night of heart-pounding indoor races on fixed bikes – was a huge draw (imagine the world's most convivial spinning class). For a while it seemed to have gone the way of bear baiting, London speedway and Music Hall, but the 21st century has seen a major revival. Expect drinking, dancing girls and a ringside seat at some truly explosive racing.

www.rollapaluza.com
www.rapha.cc

Bike Polo
One thing we love about London's bike culture is that it's from the streets up. Take Brick Lane Bike

Polo for example. Starting as a bunch of mates messing around on an East End basketball court, it's evolved into a blossoming and friendly scene. Every Sunday, teams congregate for some gently competitive messing about with mallets. Bring your bike to join in and then it's off to the Lane proper for beer and bagels.

Every Sunday, 1pm onwards in the basketball court on the corner of Brick Lane and Shacklewell Street, E2
www.bricklanebikepolo.wordpress.com

Critical Mass
Nowhere is London cyclists' mix of radical direct action and laissez-faire live-and-let-live-isms more apparent than at Critical Mass. What's it all about? No one's quite sure. Some people are here to protest climate change and congestion, some are 'reclaiming the streets' and some are just here for the vibe. Whatever your cause, there's nothing quite like setting off in your hundreds, police cars as an escort, with all of London at your feet.

6pm, last Fri of every month on the South Bank under Waterloo Bridge.
www.criticalmasslondon.org.uk

Walking the canal is like having a backstage pass to the city.

Start out on the brief five-hundred metre stretch where the Westway swoops over your head, walking down to watch the spills at the Meanwhile Gardens skatepark.

Head east through the back of the vast Paddington Basin development to Little Venice. This is picture-postcard London and a good place for brunch – wander up to Raoul's on Clifton Road.

Then there's a long sweep through the backs of the embassies that line Regent's Park, where huge gardens spill down to the waterfront, usually spookily empty bar the occasional gardener. On a summer's evening you sometimes catch a garden party here – dinner-jacketed dignitaries feeding the ducks from the jetties.

Next, head o a wonderful spot where the canal bisects the zoo. The aviary to your left, the antelopes to your right. Wait 'til dusk to come here, when the animals start making a jungle hubbub, and then make a phone call home. Wait for that inevitable "Where the hell *are* you?" (this was more fun before they moved the wolves out to Longleat).

Turn left at the floating

Chinese restaurant (whenever you see the headline 'headless corpse dredged from canal', this is the little dogleg where it normally happens), past the castle that hides the canoeing club, and on to the market.

It gets busy here – tourists eating market-stall Indonesian give way to little knots of dealers. (We don't have to tell you not to buy your drugs from guys who hang around tourist markets, do we? Good.) Keep heading east.

Now the canal is quieter – grass grows between the paving stones and you can see the occasional heron on the far bank. The new St Pancras station stretches away to the right and the boats of the King's Cross Cruising Club putter about (please don't confuse this with the King's Cross Cruise Club – gay Londoners will know that they're not the same thing at all).

Further east, cyclists give way to dog walkers and you might get the most un-Londonish "good afternoon" from a couple of people. You can head all the way into Essex, but a good stopping point is Vicky Park and a great old-school boozer – The Palm Tree.

Some people see London on an open-topped tour buses. We take the number 23.

It goes from east to west and pretty much goes past every tourist attraction on its way between Liverpool St train station and Westbourne Park. In fact, it's like driving round a Monopoly board. From Liverpool St the bus winds its way through the City, past the metal-striped skyscraper Tower 42 and the old Stock Exchange, down Threadneedle St and alongside the many-columned Bank of England. Then it's on to the portico of Mansion House (built 300 years ago for the mayor to live in) and then all the way around St Paul's Cathedral.

After that, the bus travels to:

Fleet St – where newspapers used to be written and printed, and Sweeney Todd supposedly did his dastardly deeds.

Strand – past Somerset House (home of the Royal Academy and various government offices), a church stuck in the middle of the road and Charing Cross train station, the cross being the official centre of London.

Trafalgar Square – You know the one. When you're at the bottom, look left and you can see Whitehall and the entrance to Downing Street.

Pall Mall – home to posh gentleman's clubs and the finishing line to the London Marathon. The Queen lives round the corner too.

Regent St – the first stage of one of the grandest streets in London. Look above the shop fronts at the Beaux Arts architecture in Portland stone on the upper floors.

Piccadilly Circus – not many clowns or lion tamers, but loads of bright lights and a statue that's not Eros, but is in fact his twin brother Anteros.

Then back onto **Regent St** – Hamleys the seven-storey toy store is on your right.

Oxford Circus – now we'll take a left onto Oxford Street, and after about ten minutes we'll see Selfridges on the right hand side, and some pretty fine designer shops near Bond Street station.

Park Lane – Told you it was like a Monopoly board. This is where the rich and famous hang out (mainly on the left-hand side, where Nobu and the Met Bar are).

Marble Arch – Marble Arch used to be out the front of Buckingham Palace but it was too narrow for horse and carriages to get through, so they moved it here.

Cumberland Gate – if you've been wondering, that patch of grass you've been driving next to is Hyde Park – Henry VIII's former hunting ground, and larger than the principality of Monaco. Cumberland Gate is that quite impressive looking gate thing.

Edgware Road – the smoking ban has hit some of the Middle Eastern shisha places hard, but you'll still see some people sitting outside puffing on a hubbly bubbly.

Paddington Station – This place was designed by the great engineer Isambard Kingdom Brunel. Statues dedicated to him, railway workers who died in the war, and Paddington Bear are all inside.

Kensington Park Road – Did you ever see that film Notting Hill? It was filmed round here. Keep looking on your right and you'll see Portobello Road and its market.

Golborne Road – There are two fantastic Portuguese patisseries at one end of this road, called Oporto and Lisboa. Also keep an eye out for North African shops – the street is known by some as 'Little Morocco'.

Westbourne Park Station – The end of the line. All change, please.

It's 1.15am and all's right with Soho. The kids from the suburbs and Essex are dressed up for Floridita or Punk. The bears are hanging out in front of the King's Head and the paparazzi are ensconced outside 24. Hookers rule the top end of Berwick Street, trannies rule the bottom. And at Number 9, the gallerists and cutting-room workers are getting massages. It sounds dodgy I know. A massage parlour, staffed exclusively by Thais, at the sleazy end of Brewer Street open 'til 2am. But it's not. All over Soho, people are working late nights in tiny offices and this is where they come to wash the day away.

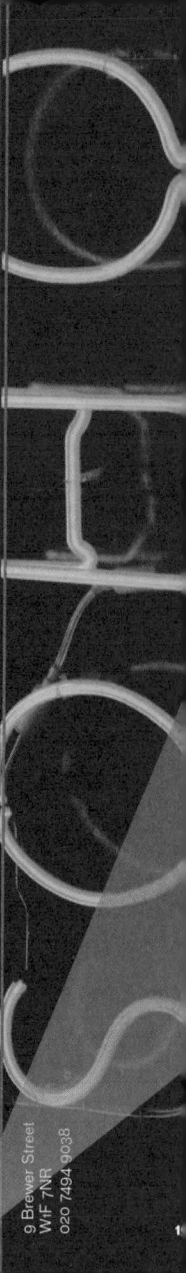

9 Brewer Street
W1F 7NR
020 7494 9038

1

There's something about Milk and Honey that puts you in a Film Noir kind of mood. Perhaps it's the entrance – an unmarked black door in the shadows at the wrong end of Poland Street.

Maybe it's the dark booths sheltering couples with their heads close together. Deals are being done, secret assignments are being made, to a soundtrack of jazz and forties standards.

Whatever it is, Milk and Honey is the kind of place where you don't feel like ordering a beer. You want something with bourbon in it. Or angostura bitters. The kind of drink you'd

Milk and Honey
61 Poland Street
W1F 7NU
www.mlkhny.com

order out the side of your mouth in a New York speakeasy. Like all genuine Noir settings, you need to know someone to get in... but if you call 07000 MLKHNY and ask to book a table, they can usually sort you out.

But if they can't...

Milk and Honey's brighter brasher little sister The Player is just round the corner. If M&H is Film Noir then this is Saturday Night Fever – noisy, messy and much easier to get into.

The Player
8-12 Broadwick Street
W1F 8HW

On the ground floor, French Grand Dames, tea-loving queens and Soho regulars soak up ornate tartes, cakes and the like with gallons of Rosie Lee. In the basement, an old peep-show has been converted into a charmingly cramped high-fashion shop. Bequiffed owner Pippa holds court over swathes of Eley Kishimoto, APC and Vivienne Westwood.

Maison Berteaux
& Shop at Maison Berteaux
27 Greek Street
W1D 5DF

Four shops, £50 in your pocket and one lunch break. Here we go.

You start in Phonica, packed with weekend DJs and bedroom mixers. It's mainly dance music, mainly electronic, but your attention is taken by a mint copy of Broselmaschine's debut album. The sleeve says: "Regarded by many as the best German folk-rock album ever!" and a quick listen on the shop's turntable suggests it's right up your strasse. You're also tempted by a Rio Balle Funk Breaks LP but there's only one copy and a cute girl's listening to it. Mental note: come back later.

12 minutes - £16.99

Across the road to Sounds Of The Universe – the home of Soul Jazz Records and the place for soul and reggae reissues and rarities. You could spend hours in here but your stomach's rumbling so just a quick browse... but there's that Compass Point compilation – Grace Jones, Talking Heads, Sly and Robbie and some great pictures and only £10.99.

22 minutes - £27.98

Back up to Harold Moore's. This might be the calmest place in W1 on a weekday lunchtime. The shop's dark and woody, the staff whisper 'hello' and there are madrigals playing quietly in the background. But Harold Moore's is pretty modernist for a classical music shop, with as much Schoenberg as Schubert, and there's a nice secondhand copy of John Cage's Four Walls with your name on it.

44 minutes - £38.97

Just time for a quick whizz round Sister Rays. It's packed with international indie kids with carrier bags filled with new purchases. You grab a smart Neon Neon picture disk – just £3.99 – but your eye is also drawn to a rare Polish pressing of Blue Monday. Never useless, but very beautiful. Never mind – the £20 tag means you haven't got enough cash anyway.

54 minutes - £40.96. Time for lunch. O: the cashpoint.

58 minutes - £60.96, and all in less than a hundred metres.

Phonica Records
51 Poland Street
W1F 7LZ
020 7025 6070
www.phonicarecords.co.uk

Sounds Of The Universe
7 Broadwick Street
W1F 0DA
020 7734 3430
www.soundsoftheuniverse.com

Harold Moore's Records
2 Great Marlborough Street
W1F 7HQ
020 7437 1576
www.hmrecords.co.uk

Sister Ray
34-35 Berwick Street
W1V 8RP
020 7734 3297
www.sisterray.co.uk

Streetartgraffitiwheatpastingstencillingculturejammingvandalismillegalpaintingtaggingpublicnuisancedefacingurban
warfarebombingartfreedomofexpressionzeitgeiststreetartgraffitiwheatpastingstencillingculturejammingvandalism
illegalpaintingtaggingpublicnuisancedefacingurbanwarfarebombingartfreedomofexpressionzeitgeist.

Whatever you call it – the works of artists like Banksy, Faile, Jamie Hewlett, Fine, Space Invader and the rest are what the public wants to see. It's all about art without boundaries – be it sprayed on a wall or some wood, pasted up in the dead of night, stuck on a building or whatever; original canvases, prints, dead phone boxes, stuffed animals, sculptures... Laz's gallery is the place to go and catch it. All the big names, as well as countless others, have had their work shown in the gallery, which used to be a porno shop in the seedier end of Soho. Duck in there to see what's fresh.

Lazarides Art Gallery
8 Greek St
W1D 4DG

Who needs the Starbucks and the S&M Cafe on Portobello Road when there's Portuguese coffee and cheap Moroccan soup on the Golborne Road? Why drink in the identikit theme bars of Upper Street when interesting independent bars keep popping up on Essex Road? And Carnaby Street's euro-trash chain stores can't hold a candle to oddities like these on Beak Street.

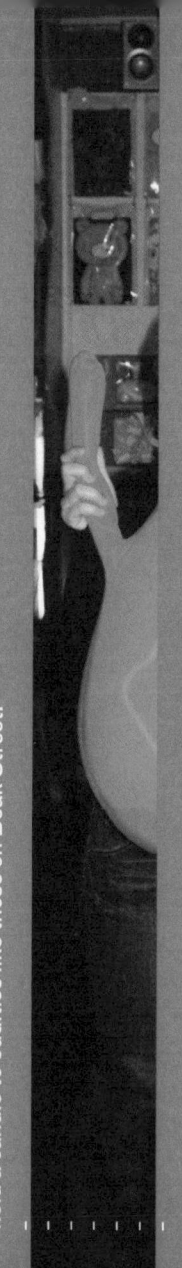

Start off at Playlounge, home to armies of designer toys, kitschy Japanese graphics and cartoon figurines (that's Barbabravo there with Yi Ying and Ice Bat alongside manger Aiden).

Playlounge
19 Beak Street
W1F 9RP
020 7287 7073

It takes a special kind of person to wear their clothes, but it's still worth having a look round Rocky Mazzilli and Louise Michielsens' Year Zero. Japanese mannequins wear original Seditionaries screenprints, skull-and-crossbones shellsuits drip with crystals, and manga scenes decorate the walls and floors.

Year Zero
37 Beak Street,
W1F 9RZ
020 7734 7727

Browse vases shaped like egg boxes and peel-off wallpaper at Do.

Do
47 Beak Street
W1F 9SE
020 7494 9090

And wind up at Riflemaker, just about the most innovative gallery space in this part of town. Don't forget to check upstairs and in the basement.

Riflemaker
79 Beak Street
W1F 9SU
020 7439 0000

From the east, you come across Friendly Society via chic coffee bars and Italian delis. From the west, it's through an alley of peep shows and adverts for "GENUIN TEEN MODLES". Perfect for a place as mixed up as this.

It's on London's seediest corner. It's a sleek little bar. It's a kind of design bar, yet with a Babycham mural and Barbies glued to the ceiling. Camp as you like, but welcoming everyone. A place to hang out... though if you're in the little bed-like booth, you're probably doing more than merely hanging out.

Mixed crowd, mixed drinks, mixed up place. Join the Society.

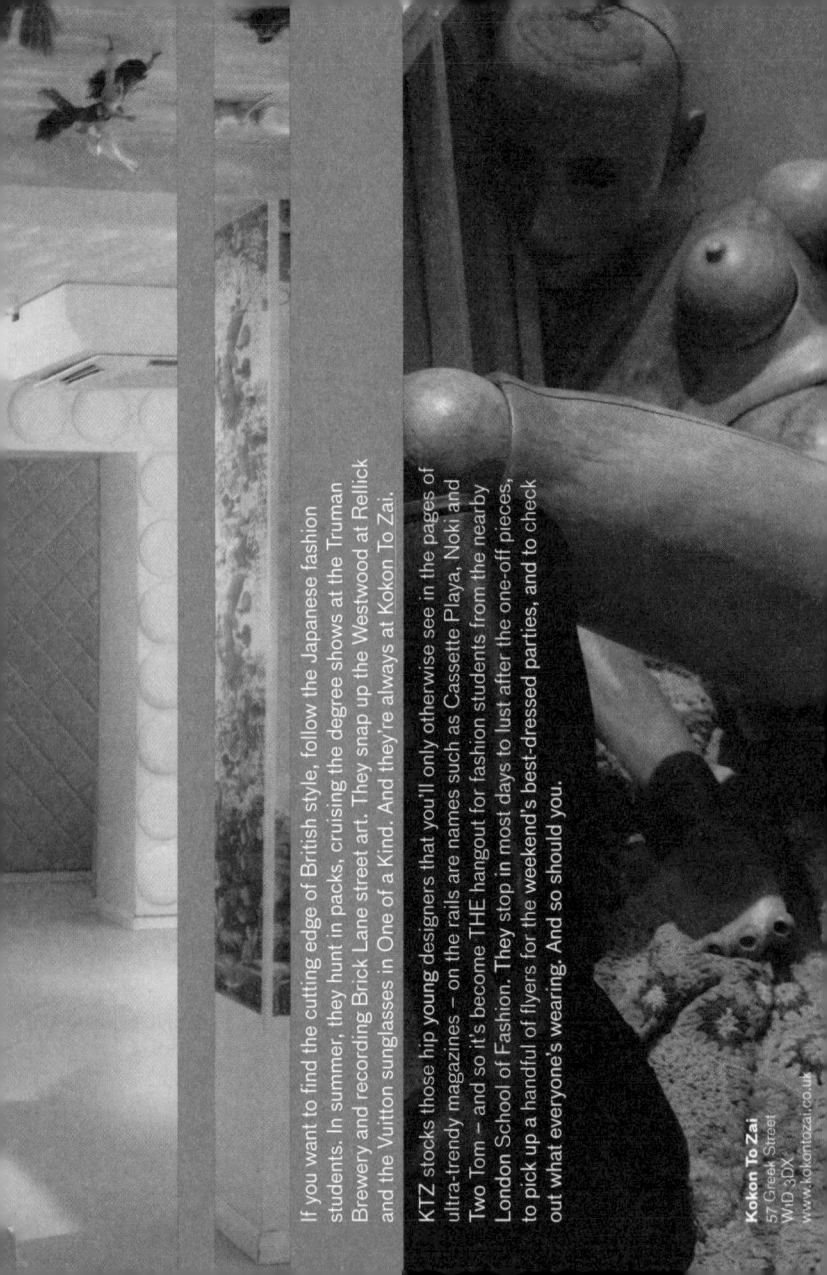

If you want to find the cutting edge of British style, follow the Japanese fashion students. In summer, they hunt in packs, cruising the degree shows at the Truman Brewery and recording Brick Lane street art. They snap up the Westwood at Rellick and the Vuitton sunglasses in One of a Kind. And they're always at Kokon To Zai.

KTZ stocks those hip young designers that you'll only otherwise see in the pages of ultra-trendy magazines – on the rails are names such as Cassette Playa, Noki and Two Tom – and so it's become THE hangout for fashion students from the nearby London School of Fashion. They stop in most days to lust after the one-off pieces, to pick up a handful of flyers for the weekend's best-dressed parties, and to check out what everyone's wearing. And so should you.

Kokon To Zai
57 Greek Street
W1D 3DX
www.kokontozai.co.uk

Mini Diamond on Berwick Street is where Dame Edna Everage buys her jewellery.

Mini Diamond
32 Berwick Street
W1F 8RL

57

Bar, members club, music venue? None of us know exactly what it is, and we don't dare ask, but we do dare slink in after pub closing for a round of Peronis in this bizarrely friendly Soho basement. Opening times seem to vary depending on the crowd, but go right after work for a guaranteed seat and some Sinatra, or late into the night to spy on the nocturnal diaspora of fifties throwbacks and confused but delighted drinkers who've been booted out of everywhere else.

Nordic Bakery design quiz

From the menus – white text in ——— font on a black background – to the cookies shaped like the cross-section of an ——— vase, everything at the Nordic Bakery has been carefully designed. The neat wooden knives and forks are by ——— and the tables and chairs are a ——— design. Even the trays are by ———. But it don't mean a thing unless the food is good. Luckily it is. The ——— is strong and hot, the ——— are little artworks in their own right and you can get that disgusting ——— that only the Scandis like.

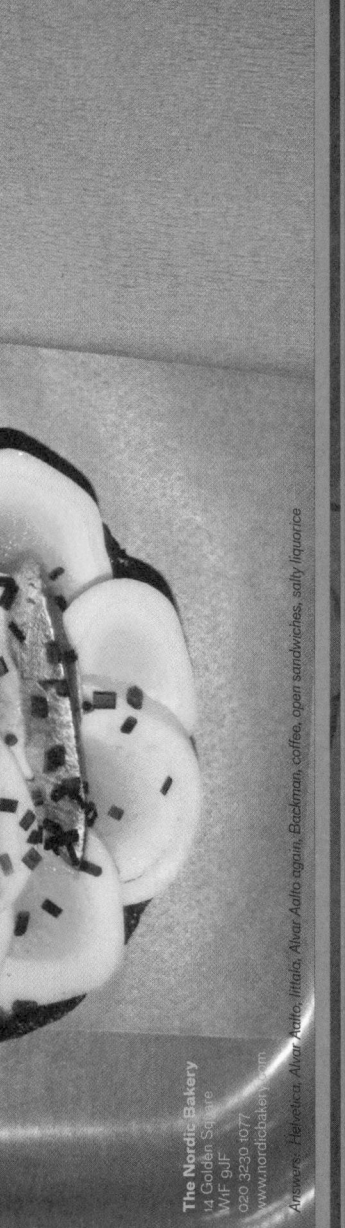

The Nordic Bakery
14 Golden Square
W1F 9JF
020 3230 1077
www.nordicbakery.com

Answers: Helvetica, Alvar Aalto, littala, Alvar Aalto again, Backman, coffee, open sandwiches, salty liquorice

If you'd taken the small alley running between Leicester Square and Chinatown early on in 1960, you'd have been confronted with a wooden scaffold around Notre Dame church. It was erected to keep the popular press away from where celebrated artist, writer and film-maker Jean Cocteau was painting a mural. In an unprepossessing alcove running along the side of the church, Cocteau created an extraordinary spectacle. A black sun shines down on a crucified Christ whose head is hidden, a rose at his feet. Romans wield spears, women weep, and right at the front is Cocteau himself. Cocteau was part of the post-war transformation of this church into one of central London's calmest and most charming spots. As you step in from scruffy old Chinatown, you're immediately confronted with Robert de Chaunac's elegant tapestry of Mary gazing over the circular chancel. Everywhere you look are other hidden artworks. Boris Anrep's elegant mosaics of 'The Pleasures of Life' line the east entrance hall, but it's the Cocteau mural that draws the visitors, who were once black-shawled French expats, but since the site got mentioned in the Da Vinci Code, are more likely to be shifty conspiracy theorists. Once you've had your fill of the mural, hunt out the statue of Our Lady of Victories in the gallery. She was beheaded in the Blitz – and the head was parachuted into Nazi-occupied Paris in 1942, so that the sculptor Henri Valette could create a new body. The finished statue was then the very first import from France to England after the war.

Notre Dame Church
Leicester Place
WC2H

Tea

Coffee

Full-fat milk

White sugar

In 1997 Hong Kong was handed back to the Chinese, ending an era of British colonial rule. But that metropolis will always remain a sister city to this big rainy one, and there's nothing more east-meets-west than Hong Kong's tea-coffee-milk drink: strong English tea, instant coffee, full-fat milk and sugar – on ice. Drink it at Jen's, accompanied with handmade Beijing dumplings and char sui noodle soup.

Jen's Café Chinatown
G/F Basement
4-8 Newport Place
WC2H 7JP

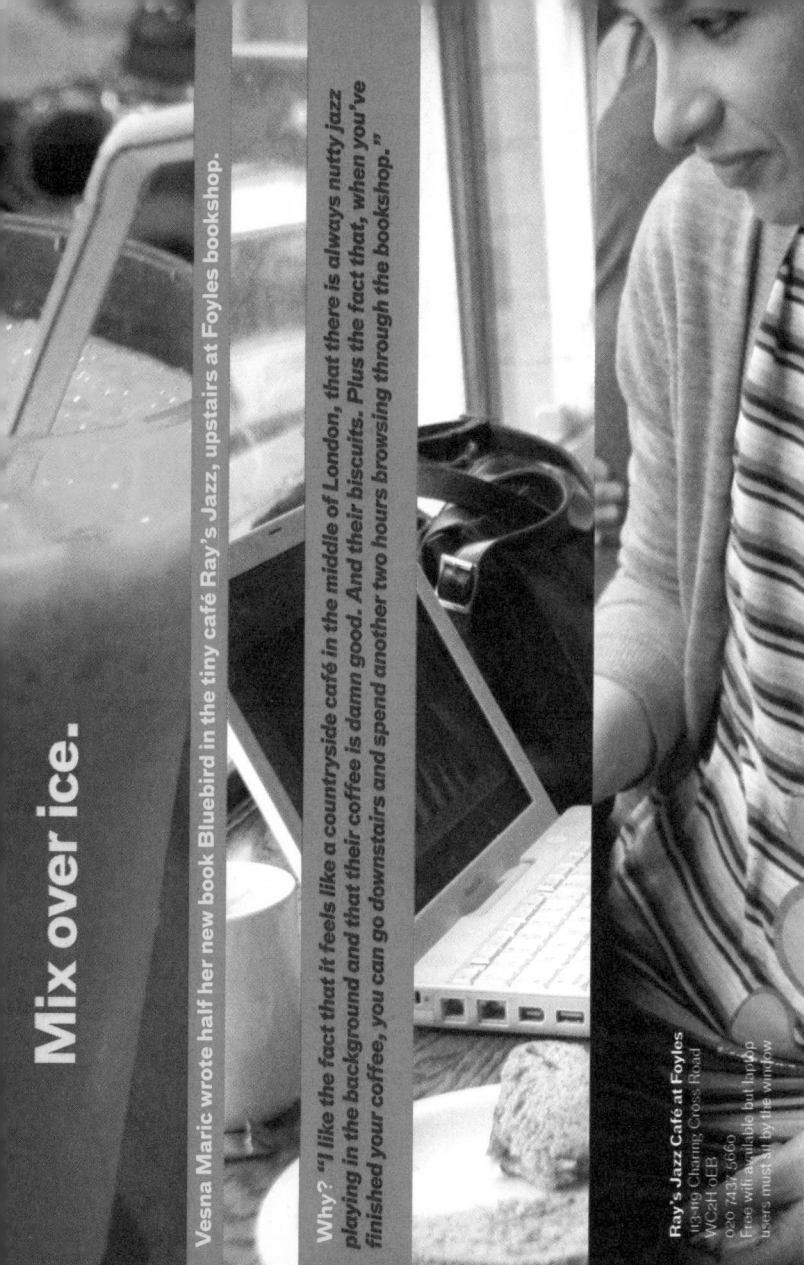

Mix over ice.

Vesna Maric wrote half her new book Bluebird in the tiny café Ray's Jazz, upstairs at Foyles bookshop.

Why? *"I like the fact that it feels like a countryside café in the middle of London, that there is always nutty jazz playing in the background and that their coffee is damn good. And their biscuits... Plus the fact that, when you've finished your coffee, you can go downstairs and spend another two hours browsing through the bookshop."*

Ray's Jazz Café at Foyles
113-119 Charing Cross Road
WC2H 0EB
020 7437 5660
Free wifi available but laptop
users must sit by the window

Getting your nails done, a waxing and a complicated facial can be a slap in the wallet for the mostly skint. Fortunately, the London School of Beauty's Esthetique salon offers all the above at pocket-money prices. It uses OPI colours applied by experienced trainees, while

strains of classical music and stringent tutor checks help you relax into the whole experience. If you're glowing with a love for all humanity afterwards, there's a Blood Donor centre across the road.

Sigh. Then again, price exists for a reason and occasionally throwing money at a problem can be the quickest and best way to feel completely gorgeous and spoiled. Instead of forking out £13 for Chanel's lumpy Rouge Noir, head to Kingly Court and check into the Beauty

Lounge, a 1940s sanctuary in the middle of tourist hell. Their Ole Henriksen £30 express facial will have your skin as sexy as Rita in 30 minutes flat, and at £25, their Brazilian is the probably cheapest in town that doesn't remove both your skin and your will to live.

London School of Beauty
First Floor
47-50 Margaret Street
W1W 8SB
020 7636 1893

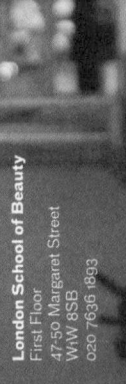

The Beauty Lounge
1 Kingly Court
W1B 5PW
020 7734 6161

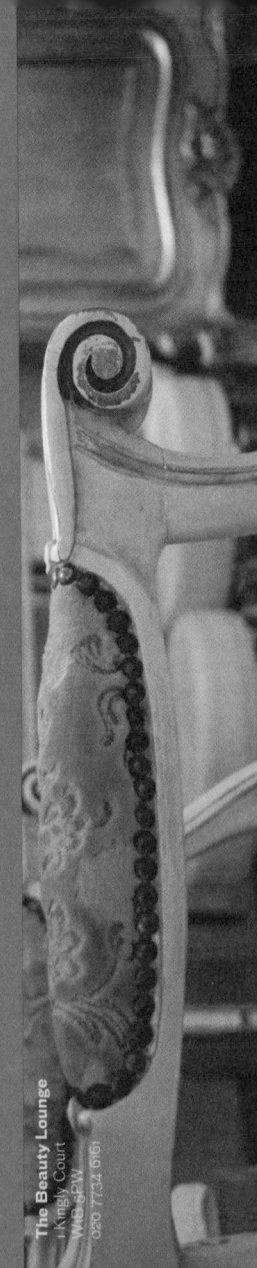

... turn left out of the Beauty Lounge into Kingly Court. This was once where Soho's grime collided with Regent Street's glitz. Home to the Pinstripe Club, where John Profumo first met Christine Keeler, the court is now a smart three-story plaza filled with shops and cafés. It's a nouveau Mod hang-out – Fred Perry, Lambretta and Ben Sherman are all here – and even the secondhand shops are packed with button-down shirts and pork-pie hats. It's also home to a growing wave of modern-not-mod new designers. Our favourite is t-shirt specialist Super Superficial. Row upon row of nothing but t-shirts by cool young illustrators. This is the place hip London souvenir hunters are heading.

Super Superficial
Kingly Court
Kingly Street, W1B 5PW
www.Supersuperficial.com

On a regular evening down The Phoenix you'll find

- Actors from the theatre upstairs having a swift one before curtain-up.
- Actors who aren't in the play upstairs waiting until the first lot have gone onstage before bitching about them.
- The Manager perched on a stool at the end of the bar, making sure that the crisps are served in a bowl.
- A nervous first-time journalist interviewing the support band for whoever's playing at the Astoria across the road.
- One goth.
- Savvy clubbers taking advantage of the only West End bar where you don't have to queue for a beer.
- One bunch of girls in feather boas singing along to the showtunes.
- And any real Londoner who's ever had to find a place for ten people to meet in town.

Nominally a member's bar, they're notoriously slack. Get here before 8pm and add yourself to the list above...

We call it The Phoenix, but others call it Shuttleworth's, I've heard it called the Theatre Bar and its actual title is the Noel Coward Bar.

The Phoenix
110 Charing Cross Road
WC2H oJP

It's like a department store for the cool kids. Packed with the beautiful (ceramic boomboxes, Perspex stag's heads, top-hat lampshades), the fashionable (one-off outfits from new designers straight from art schools and fashion colleges) and the useful (books, clocks, "wake me up at Brixton" Tube stickers), Beyond The Valley is a one-stop crash course in everything hip London has to offer.

Oh and it's an art gallery too...

Beyond The Valley
2 Newburgh Street
W1F 7RD

So where do bartenders drink?

We asked Julian de Nechaud de Feral (see page 248) where the experts get their alcoholic kicks in the West End.

"If I am in Soho feeling lonesome and blue, and I'm after a great cocktail made by a friendly, unpretentious team in an upbeat environment, it would have to be the favourite age-old combo of Lab and The Player. In between the two I occasionally duck into the bowels of La Floridita to drool over their expansive rum selection and have a swift one of what they do best – a daiquiri. Maybe even a Floridita daiquiri if the ghost of Hemingway is hovering close by.

For something with a touch more of a sophisticated environment and good live jazz to match, Ronnie Scott's. After all that jazz, if I can still manage to slur "innish an' Gunn" (a great beer aged in bourbon barrels) and "shootch chasher pleesh", I might find myself stumbling down to Trafalgar Square to hide in one of Doon's caves, below the Albannach.

If I'm dressed to the nines, I've saved up my lunch money and I'm looking to impress, I'd do a hotel bar crawl, starting with the sexy newly-refurbed Artesian bar at the Langham Hotel, where Alex always looks after me. Then south a bit to Calabrese's bar at 50 St. James's to greedily stuff myself with yummy complimentary vegetable chips and be satiated by Salvatore, Steve and Raffaello's exemplary service and charm. Finally on to the King of Old School London Hotel Bars, Dukes Hotel, where head bartender Alessandro mixes the most dangerous diamond martinis (vodka/gin frozen, poured straight out the bottle) in town. After that you really should be going home sir.

Lab
12 Old Compton Street,
W1D 4TQ, 020 7437 7820

The Player
8-12 Broadwick Street,
W1F 8HW, 020 7494 9125

La Floridita
100 Wardour Street,
W1F 0TN, 020 7314 4000

Ronnie Scott's
47 Frith Street,
W1D 4HT, 020 7439 0747

Artesian
Langham Hotel
1C Portland Place,
W1B 1JA, 020 7636 1000

Fifty
50 St James's Street
SW1A 1JT
0870 415 5050

Dukes Hotel
St. James's Place
SW1A 1NY
020 7491 4840

Could it be that the 200-odd metres of Hanway Street are more fun than the mile-and-a-half of Oxford Street?

First off there's the mighty Bradley's Spanish Bar – the spot for that post-work, pre-gig, 'I'm-not-paying-four-quid-for-a-lager-at-the-Astoria-let's-get-a-couple-in-here' drink. On summer evenings, the crowds spill out into the street, while the toilets downstairs are full of guys changing out of their work trousers and girls doing their make-up (and occasionally vice versa). It's also the only place I've seen a fist-fight break out over whose turn it is on the jukebox. They take their music seriously here.

20

As they do further down the street at JB's and On The Beat, proper afternoon-wasting vinyl useums. Best to shop here and then get a drink at Bradley's, the other way round can prove expensive.

If it's 9.30pm, then there's flamenco at the Costa Dorada, if it's later you might have to look for one of the street's hidden all-night drinking holes cough – above the camera shop – cough.

COSTA DORA

And at the end – policed by some serious bouncers – is Hakkasan. It's not London's only Michelin-starred Chinese) but a basil martini up at the bar is an indulgence we all deserve sometimes.

While Oxford Street is named for its destination (yawn), Hanway Street is named after the eccentric Jonas Hanway (1712–1786), renowned for being the first man in London to carry an umbrella – a decision that rather splendidly had cabbies trying to "hoot and hustle him down". He also opposed the drinking of tea, calling it "this flatulent liquor", and he was buried in his stilts.

info@costadoradarestaurant.co.uk.

www.costadoradarestaurant.co

Live FLAMENCO SHOWS
Tue–Thur 9:30 pm
Frid–Sat 10:00 pm

Tattoos and torch songs, sequins and cigars. Dressed-up girls and messed up-boys.

Welcome to the Soho of old.

Where the streets meet the galleries there is Cosh.

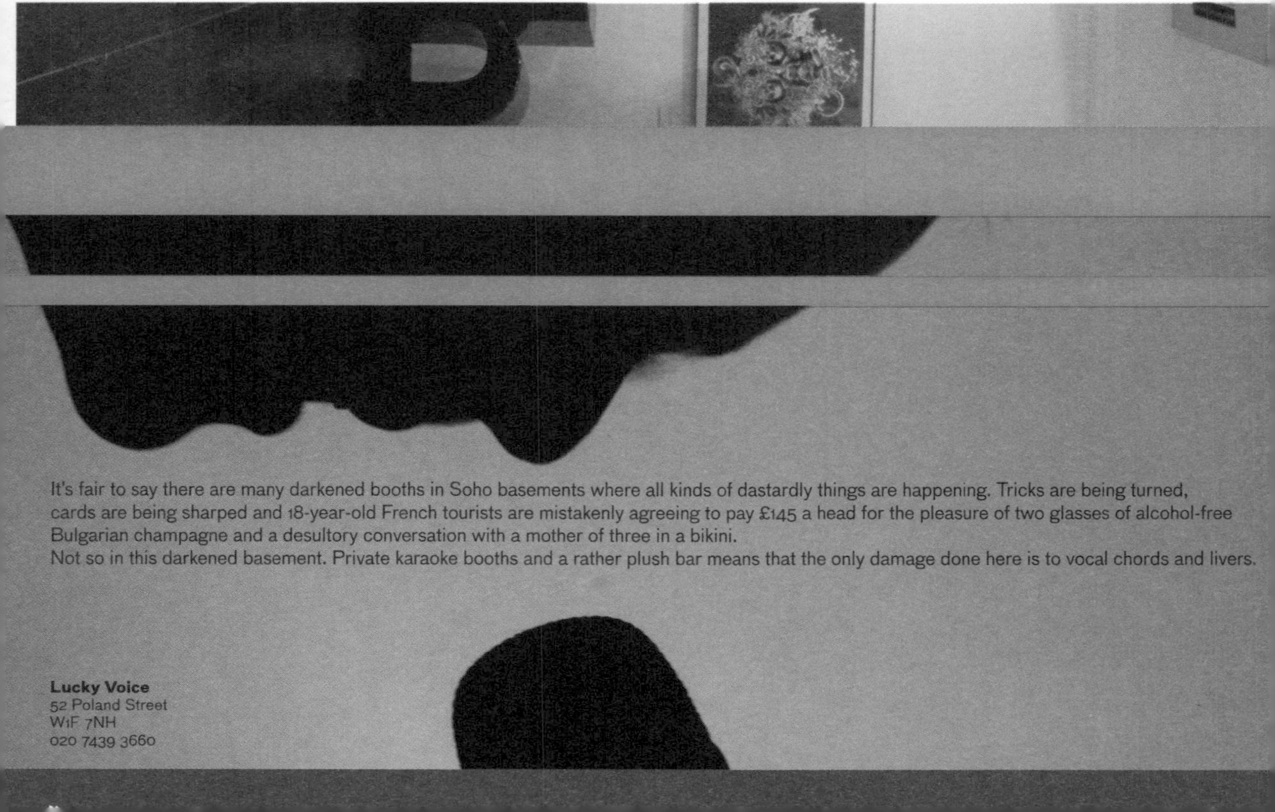

It's fair to say there are many darkened booths in Soho basements where all kinds of dastardly things are happening. Tricks are being turned, cards are being sharped and 18-year-old French tourists are mistakenly agreeing to pay £145 a head for the pleasure of two glasses of alcohol-free Bulgarian champagne and a desultory conversation with a mother of three in a bikini.

Not so in this darkened basement. Private karaoke booths and a rather plush bar means that the only damage done here is to vocal chords and livers.

Lucky Voice
52 Poland Street
W1F 7NH
020 7439 3660

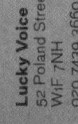

This beautiful World Clock is tucked away in Piccadilly Tube station. Just thought you'd like to know.

THE WORLD TIME TODAY

PR agency Margaret meets in Soho's rather lovely Breakfast Club.

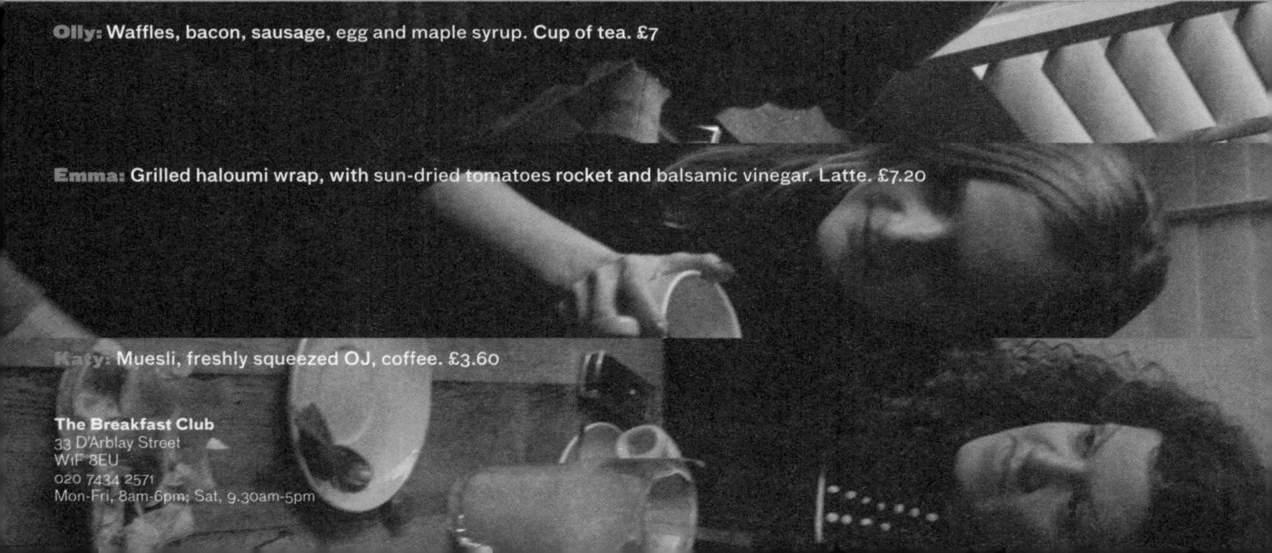

Olly: Waffles, bacon, sausage, egg and maple syrup. Cup of tea. £7

Emma: Grilled haloumi wrap, with sun-dried tomatoes rocket and balsamic vinegar. Latte. £7.20

Katy: Muesli, freshly squeezed OJ, coffee. £3.60

The Breakfast Club
33 D'Arblay Street
W1F 8EU
020 7434 2571
Mon-Fri, 8am-6pm; Sat, 9.30am-5pm

Broccoli and sausage? The queues start forming about 11.45am, with people craning their necks to see what the specials are. **Artichoke?** Whatever they are, they're going to be in the form of greasy, spicy, loaded-with-toppings, Roman-style pizzas. **Potato with fontina?** Think fast, turn off your mobile (or risk a full-on strop from the Italian owners), and make your choice. **Courgette and goat's cheese?** Perhaps you should get a couple of slices.

Malleti
26 Noel Street
W1F 8GT
020 7439 4096
Mon-Sat 10am-5pm

Ever met a mean vegetarian? They're just predisposed to niceness, with a warmth and respect for all sentient beings. So the friendly service at Beatroot is almost a given. Getting food is as plain as a cucumber: you pick a small, medium or large box that they fill to the brim with your choice of any of ten hot and ten cold dishes. We defy you to eat more than a medium box, especially when the chef comes out and keeps on cramming it in because 'you've got to try a bit of this, man'. Add to this a tasty range of juices and smoothies, vegan desserts and the fact that it's easily the cheapest decent eat in Soho, and even non-veggies will leave happy. A gorgeous and guilt-free eating experience.

This bit of Old Compton Street starts to get a bit wishy-washy; crap-ass fashion meccas and the dregs of Shaftesbury and Wardour's duller ends. However, this caffeine-fuelled haven will sharpen your brain for under a quid, for under a quid with perhaps the City's best value espresso and cappuccino. Standing room only, but chances are that if you sat down to drink this coffee you'd vibrate off the seat.

Beatroot
92 Berwick Street
W1F OQD
020 7437 8591
Mon-Fri 9am-9pm
Sat 11am-9pm
www.beatroot.org.uk

Algerian coffee House
52 Old Compton Street
W1D 4PB
020 1437 2480

Wimbledon Stadium
Plough Lane
SW17
7.30am-12.30pm every Saturday
£2 before 8.30am, 50p after
Cars £10, vans £20
01932 355 538

Sometimes it's not the buying, it's the browsing.

Sotheby's is the best free gallery in London. An ever-changing line-up of million-pound artworks, a great café and no obligation to buy.

There's a different kind of pleasure to be found browsing at the car boot sale – it ought to be all about unearthing bargains but half the joy is just seeing what kind of old tat people have had clogging up their houses all these years...

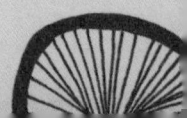

Car boots vs Collectors

Sotheby's
34-35 New Bond Street
W1S 2RT
020 7293 5000

Soho Square
W1

Soho Square might be a scrubby little handkerchief of grass populated by bike messengers and teenagers sneaking puffs on joints, but if you grab a coffee from Flat White and find a free bench you have a view of the whole of London city life passing by..

...but Epping Forest is London's little secret. 6,000 acres of woodland, badgers and deer and the best walking and mountain biking for miles.

MODELS

XXX

2

The Square vs The Forest

Epping Forest
Epping, Theydon Bois
or Debden Tube

South

Small but perfectly formed, this conversion of a 16th-century barn – once the site of a banquet for Elizabeth I and her alchemist among others – crams a lot into its four tiny rooms.

Couples canoodle in the boudoirish dining room while local hipsters booze, dance and chat in the elegant downstairs bar. Several punters have claimed to see a spectral figure on the upstairs landing – either the ghost of a local flower seller or the effect of one too many Amaretto Sours.

Lost Society
697 Wandsworth Road
SW8 3JF
020 7652 6526

Once upon a time,

not too long ago, two guys opened a bakery in Clapham. They decided to make amazing sourdough breads and all kinds of other nice stuff. And lots of people visited every day.

Queues formed, so they put out a toaster so that people could snack while they waited.

And the queues got longer so they put in a couple of tables and chairs, and they were full every day, but everyone still wanted the toast so they put a snazzy Dualit toaster on every table.

And without really trying they had a cool little café to go along with the bakery, and they even started making their own marmalade.

And so it came to pass that people came in and paid pennies to make their own toast and drink tea and buy bread for later.

And they all lived happily ever after.

Breads Etc
127 Clapham High Street
SW4 7SS
020 7720 3601
www.breadsetcetera.com
Tue-Sat, 10am-10pm
Sun, 10am-4pm

From a seat in the snug you can see:

A surfboard
Spiderman in a hammock
A blowtorch (broken)
A sign to Bordeaux
Eight ladles
Woodworking tools
A cut-out Frank Sinatra
Traffic lights
A lobster in a cage
A Chinese lantern
A box kite
A miniature tambourine
Two tea trays
and a cloth boat

It's fair to say that the owners of the Prince of Wales pub don't care much for the minimalist school of bar design. Instead, the pub that newcomers call POW! (because of the neon sign outside), and locals call the Full Of Crap (see list above), is a straightforward, pint-and-a-packet-of-crisps local, and the ideal place to start a Clapham pub crawl.

Prince of Wales
38 Clapham Old Town
SW4 0LB
020 7622 3530

It's all very New York.

The lights are low, the walls are bare stone, the barmen are attentive. You order a mojito and choose a funky chair by the curved floor-to-ceiling window. Soft music plays as you gaze out over ~~dreamy skyscrapers and a low-hanging mist on the Hudson River~~ Poundstretcher and Nando's. Oh well, the illusion may not be complete, but this is still a gem of a bar on a street filled with chain bars and unfriendly pubs.

The Loft
67 Clapham High St
SW4 7TG
It's not the easiest place to
find – look out for the bouncer
lounging in a doorway just to
the right of Tesco

Some people diss Clapham.

Some people are dimwitted and ignorant. SW4 harbours not only London's finest breakfast venues, but also Gastro, a rackety little hutch of louche French wood with a seriously good line in steak. Favoured by restless artists and writers during the day, at night it bustles with savvy locals, and lovers of a good yarn and much, much red wine.

Gastro
67 Venn Street
SW4 0BD
020 7627 0222

Alas, like most sacred things in life, all the best gay parties have succumbed to the law of gravity, and migrated south.

Heaven's rumoured imminent closure (as we write this) only strengthens the fact that the Vauxhall's fast-spreading Gay Village, or 'Voho', is challenging for Soho's crown.

Vauxhall offers a diverse scene from leather clubs like The Hoist to cabaret bars and clubs like the Dame of Vauxhall herself, the Royal Vauxhall Tavern. If drag shows and fetish clubs aren't your thing then you'll probably be found in one of the two party juggernauts Fire and Area. Or, since as they are but a short hop, skip and jump away from each other, both.

Area is a recent addition to the Vauxhall Village, and it has everything required for the sophisticated gay clubber. With an extreme makeover that would make Carol Smillie grimace, the club now features two packed dance floors, six bars, luxuriously comfy chillout areas, sumptuous chandeliers and a jaw-dropping light and laser set up that could probably bleach your teeth if it pointed in the wrong direction. Juicy Resident DJs Steve Pitron and The Oli spin feel-good funky house and the latest electro beats, while you shimmy between old friends and hopefully some hot new ones.

This club has already hosted huge international parties from Space,

Toybox and Billy, and it's easy to see why. This is state-of-the-art clubbing, where decadence meets debauchery.

When you're all warmed up, its time to move on to where it doesn't get any hotter: the world-infamous disco inferno Fire. Horny homos, Brazilian beefcakes and tasty twinks from a million different places converge here to party like it's the last night on earth. This is hardcore clubbing at its best and Fire's international reputation is truly deserved.

The "pull out all the stops" party production is faultless, keeping the crowd going for dangerously long all-nighters with an unrivalled atmosphere. An impressive roster of superstar DJs including The Sharp Boys, Stevie B and Terry Bryan make it near impossible to resist the urge to whip off your top and lose yourself in the crowds, all the while surrounded by London's hottest tottie in four fabulous archways of disco delight.

If all that has left you wanting yet more, peel yourself a party segment that refreshes bits that no other clubs can reach by heading back to Fire for the naughtiest Sunday night party of all, <u>Orange</u>. This is simply the fruitiest way to finish off the weekend and turn Monday morning monotony into a melange of Ibiza-style minimal messiness and proper funked-up tunes.

This sweaty adrenaline-busting after-hours session, with its Adonis-like GoGos and the most up-for-it crowd in London, is the hideout of hardcore clubbers and strict devotees of hedonism... plus all those who will call in sick the next day.

Royal Vauxhall Tavern
372 Kennington Lane
SE11 5HY
www.theroyalvauxhalltavern.co.uk

Hoist
Arch 47b & 47c
South Lambeth Road
SW8
www.thehoist.co.uk

Fire
38-42 Parry Street
020 7820 0550
www.fireclub.co.uk

Area
67-68 Albert Embankment
SE1 7TP
0871 971 4533
www.areaclub.info

Some bands that have played here that you might have heard of:
Archie Bronson Outfit
Architecture In Helsinki
Biffy Clyro
The Black Lips
Bloc Party
Brakes
British Sea Power
Broken Family Band
Bromheads Jacket
Castanets
Clor
The Cribs
Daniel Johnston
Die! Die! Die!
Do Me Bad Things
Dogs
Duke Special
Duke Spirit
The Enemy

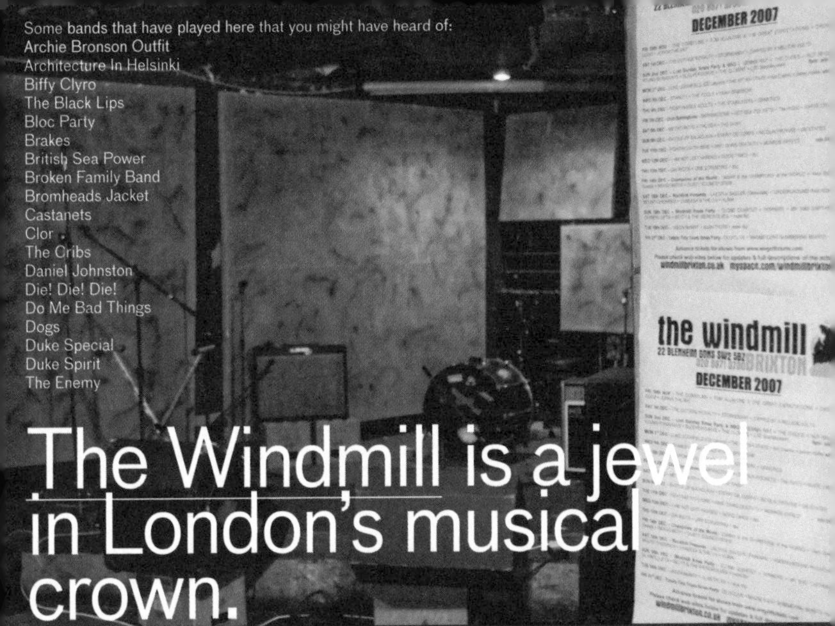

The Windmill is a jewel in London's musical crown.

Found at the end of an anonymous road in Brixton, it's an essential stop for any band that wants to make it big. It's got live music seven nights a week, so chances are you're gonna stumble across something great. And it's cheap, dirt cheap, to get in. As in less than a fiver. It's like some kind of lo-fi, scruffy bastard of a musical grotto.

The Windmill
22 Blenheim Gardens
SW2 5BZ
www.windmillbrixton.co.uk

Guillemots
Get Cape Wear Cape Fly
Hard-Fi
Hot Chip
The Horrors
The Howling
Jamie T
Jeremy Warmsley
Klaxons
Kurt Wagner (Lambchop)
Ali Love
Mates Of State
Maximo Park
Noah & The Whale
OK Go
The Pipettes
Plan B
Pop Levi
The Rakes
Rumble Strips
Scritti Politti
Scouting For Girls
Shitdisco
The Spinto Band
The Sunshine Underground
Television Personalities
Tilly & The Wall
Tom McRae
Tom Vek
Tim Wheeler (Ash)
The View
The Wombats
Yeasayer
The Young Knives

Brixton gets a bad rap. Even those who don't openly badmouth it raise their eyebrows when I inform them of my neighbourhood of choice. And that's just fine, because it means I'm more likely to find an empty table at the Ritzy Picturehouse, where wifi is free and hot chocolate abundant. As a wannabe screenwriter, their café, set among the packed screens, makes for great inspiration.

Ritzy Picturehouse
Coldharbour Lane
SW2 1JG
0871 704 2065

Plan B
418 Brixton Road
SW9 7AY
020 7733 0926

It's 5pm on a Friday evening and you're out of work early

In Brixton Market everything's peachy – housewives in hats are picking up pig's trotters for their tea, porters are pushing shopping trolleys of fresh pork for the early evening rush. You grab a patty from the Roy on the corner, maybe a mix-tape for later - you're having a night in tonight.

...but at Charles's stall in the arches you meet the girl/boy of your dreams. No problem, <u>Plan B</u>'s just round the corner

Dex
467-469 Brixton Road
SW9 8HH
0871 971 3844

and it's two-for-one beers before the bands come on...

Then it's "fancy some dinner? I know a little place."

And what a little place. <u>Upstairs</u> has no sign, doesn't advertise, doesn't make a fuss. Hidden away above an anonymous coffee-shop on Acre Lane, it's what every neighbourhood needs. A smart little French restaurant-cum-late-night bar with good food and decent wines.

So it's time to make your move... ask the question... if you get a 'yes' then it's on to <u>Dex</u> – you've gotta love

Upstairs
89B Acre Lane
SW2 5TN
020 7733 8855

Brixton's own design hotel. A late
licence, a hot-tub on the roof and
seriously cool just-for-the-night rooms.
And if he/she says no?
There's always...

Speedy Noodles
506-508 Brixton Road
SW9 7AW
020 7326 4888

Sometimes
the city tells
you where to
go.

Sun and Doves
61-63 Coldharbour Lane
SE5 9NS
020 7733 1525

GX Gallery
43 Denmark Hill
SE5 8SR
020 7703 8395

Dark Horse
16 Grove Lane
SE5 8SY

We start with a quick pint in the Sun and Doves – HQ for local artists and film-makers, and the only place we know where you can drink almond milk and watch Sunday afternoon flicks on the big screen. The guy behind the bar says that, though the artists on their walls are pretty cool, there's even better at GX down the road.

So we head that way, and the chap at GX says "I've had people come in for a card and walk out with a seven-grand painting". There's great stuff in here – low-life South London scenes like some kind of cockney Beryl Cook, playful little sculptures and, set into the floor, a painting that paradoxically doubled in value when John Lennon defaced it after a fight with the artist. We also learn that another of their artists is gutted; he's spent the best part of a year working on an Iraqi car-bomb piece – now Mark Wallinger's come up with the same idea for the fourth plinth.

We feel like another drink. The bloke at GX recommends the Dark Horse – a darkly elegant little place – but the garden at Seymour Bros is a distraction. A quick cuppa out back, feeling all Dickensian, and then a Leffe in the Horse. A man at the bar is staying at the Church Street Hotel –

"you've got to see it" he says.
It's only across the road.

And he's right - you do have to
see it. An anonymously hip façade
hides a riot of Spanish colour.
Rooms are deep blue or green,
dotted with cubbyholes hiding
skeletons and ceramic saints.
By each bed is a selection of
paperbacks (Bukowski, Huxley,
Hunter S. Thompson) and a lone
rose in an empty tequila bottle.
Jose behind the counter won't
have his picture taken until he's got
his flowery shirt on and a Jesus
figurine.

It's dinnertime now, and Jose
recommends La Moon, so it's
back up Denmark Hill. Jose says
it's Chinese. The waitress says
"The owners are from Vietnam,
via China, the chef's Malaysian.
We just cook anything that tastes
good." Indeed they do. The
soft-shell crabs are a greasy joy
and the fiery soups are a meal in
themselves. The waitress says
there's a Thai drinking den up the
road but it's hard to find. Easier
is The Crypt – you'll find flyers
everywhere for this jazz club under
a church. And from there, who
knows? If you let it, Camberwell
has its own ideas about how you
should travel through its streets.
Open your mind, open your ears
and enjoy the journey.

Until you've seen Judy Finnegan quaff
deep from a mug shaped like a huge
stone head then you've never really known
horror. Sarf London's most unexpected
bar (and ex-Richard and Judy occasional
hangout) is a riot of tiki masks, fresh fruity
cocktails and tribal beats. Don't worry –
Judy doesn't drink there any more.

South London Pacific
340 Kennington Road
SE11 4LD
020 7820 9189
www.southlondonpacific.com
Fri and Sat nights only

Imagine your dream café

Y'know, the one that'd be downstairs from your flat in an ideal world. What's it like? Maybe a little bit old-fashioned, charmingly weather-beaten – a cross between an old friend's kitchen and a particularly well-stocked bric-a-brac shop?

Perhaps run by Italians who know their macchiatos from their espressos?

How about populated with locals who table-hop to say hi to the neighbours?

And home to an imperious and slovenly cat.

Second Floor, 132 Lower Marsh is currently occupied. Damn them.

Scooterworks
132 Lower Marsh
SE1 7AE
020 7620 1421
Mon-Sat 10am-6pm

Radio Days
87 Lower Marsh
SE1 7AB
020 7928 0800

What The Butler Wore
131 Lower Marsh
SE1 7AE
020 7261 1353

Marie's
90 Lower Marsh
SE1 7AB
020 7928 1050

Crockatt and Powell
119-120 Lower Marsh
SE1 7AE
020 7928 0234

The whole of Lower Marsh seems to be made up of the kinds of shops it'd be good to live above. There's What The Butler Wore – distinctly a cut above your average vintage store with handmade cards and a battered jukebox so you'd always have something elegant to wear.

You'd need a bookshop. An independent bookshop. And Crockatt and Powell has everything you need; whip-smart assistants who can rattle on about Faulkner for days, some great bargains and a blog so enthusiastic that it'll have you spending like there's no tomorrow.

And there's Marie's. In an ideal world every street would have a Marie's. By day a salt-of-the-earth greasy spoon. Nothing fancy, just eggs/chips/beans/sausage/bacon or combinations of the above. With tea. By night it fills with local Asian kids and serves dirt-cheap dead-good Thai food. It still looks like a caff – but it tastes amazing.

(Oh and there's Radio Days – to be honest you don't *need* a shop that sells glorious old tech like pre-war viewfinders and Bakelite radios, but they're just about the most enthusiastic people you'll ever meet. Go say hello.)

We mentioned to Julian, bartender at Flaxon Ptootch (*see page 142*) that we were going to use a picture of a Waterloo sunset as the back page of the book, and that it was a real shame that the cocktail of the same name was so unpleasant. Someone ought to come up with a better one, we mused.

A week later we got this recipe in our inbox.

50ml Beefeater gin
50ml fresh orange juice
50ml fresh pink or red grapefruit juice
10ml Grand Marnier orange Curaçao
10ml sugar syrup
1 dash Bitter Truth Old-Time aromatic bitters
50 ml POM Wonderful pomegranate juice

Fill a Collins glass (long glass, about 12-14 ounces capacity) with cubed ice, shake the first six ingredients and strain into glass. Gently pour the pomegranate juice into the glass, and top with a chunky slice of red grapefruit (aka 'sunrise' grapefruit).

Here he is making it. His gift to us, and ours to you.

tinyurl.com/46tn8a
tinyurl.com/2z86b

About le cool

le cool is about loving life and living love.

We are passionate about uncovering the best in the city, from an amazing meal to a special event, and then sharing what we've learnt. We don't care about the hippest or the latest, we want to hunt down the most incredible experiences we can find.

le cool started in 2003 as a Barcelona weekly email magazine, a funky agenda and a guide to the city's cultural life, a good friend who's always in the know. Now we publish email magazines in eight cities around Europe, to 180,000 readers. This is just the beginning. And we never, ever accept payment or favours in return for content.

Visit www.lecool.com to sign up.

le cool cities:
Amsterdam, Barcelona, Istanbul, Lisbon, London, Madrid, Milan, Rome

le cool books:
Amsterdam, Barcelona, Lisbon, London (in English) Madrid (in Spanish)

Credits

Editor: Mat Osman
Designer: Jeremy Leslie
Design assistant: Joel Ng

Founder/Managing director: René Lönngren
Editorial director: Andrew Losowsky
Production: Olivier Talbot

Writers
Jim Batty
Sarah Bee
Kat Brown
David Barnett
Guy Bingley
Alana Cassidy
Craig Clark
Eamon Downes
Dominic Edney
Roxy Erickson
Nick Fallowfield-Cooper
Jessica Gearheart
Jo Gifford
Alcuin Hacker
Delaina Haslam
Lara Kavanagh
Josh Jones
Vesna Maric
Hannah Marshall
Ian Marshall
Marcie MacLellan
Chloe McCloskey
Tom Medwell
Julian de Nechaud de Feral
Lauren Nightingale
Mat Osman
Emma Pettit
John Power
Remi Rough
Shanthi Sivanesan
Terence Teh
Sarah Vianney
Sophie Walker
Herbert Wright

Photographers
Jim Batty
Rafael Estefania
Nick Fallowfield-Cooper
Ben Hammersley
Hunter-Li
Paul Khera
Mat Osman
Chloe McCloskey
Tom Medwell
Joel Ng
Shanthi Sivanesan
Tim White
Dragon pictures from
www.jimbatty.com
London map from
www.openstreetmap.org

Illustrators
Toby Pennington/YCN
Remi Rough
Jim Stoten /Heart
Therese Vandling

Index

Pubs, bars and clubs

Hairdressers cum art galleries that turn into clubs in the evening

Art and Culture

Skyscrapers

Where to eat

Cafes with fetish shops in their basements

Places to stay

Activities

This has been a catalogue of remarkable experiences. To find other ways to navigate this book and share your experiences, visit www.lecool.com/books/london/more